A B C

of a

medieval

church

In memory of AEHC
whose knowledge, love and care for
churches, bells and organs
was exemplary

ISBN 9780956710253

First published in 2018
by
At the Sign of the Pipe

Design and typesetting by Jonathan Foxwood
Printing pre-production by David Shuker

Printed in Great Britain by Anchorprint, Syston, Leicestershire

Front cover : Maidstone in Kent
Kerfons chapel near Lannion in northern Brittany
Salle in Norfolk
plan overlay : Heckington in Lincolnshire
Rear cover : Thaxted in Essex

Photographs on front and rear covers
(c) Vicki Harding

CONTENTS

ILLUSTRATIONS

COLOUR PLATES with captions, between pages 54 and 55

SOURCES OF BLACK AND WHITE ILLUSTRATIONS
Introduction : St Buryan, Cornwall
Quire stalls Gamlingay, Cambs (S & N windows, and S low
     window inside & outside) & New College, Oxford
     (steps)
The chancel door Frampton, Lincs
Seats for mass celebrants Thompson, Norfolk

Lighting the sanctuary Southwold, Suffolk
Lavabos Blockley, Glos
Stobbes Dorchester, Oxon
Easter Sepulchres Kelling, Norfolk
Squints Irthlingborough, Northants
Tabernacles Duxford (St John), Cambs
Pyxes Dennington, Suffolk
Tiles Salle. Norfolk
Retables and mensa slabs Ulcombe, Kent (Lady chapel) &
        Warmington, Oxon (vestry)
Brass and brasses Chipping Campden, Gloucs
North-east buildings :
Bassingbourn, Cambs (outside evidence of former building)
Noseley Leics (engraving of tower, two-storey sacristy etc.,
        attached to north side of private college chapel, from
        Nichols' *Leicestershire,* 1792 ; demolished early C19)
Hillesden, Bucks (NE building *c*1490, with elegant turret)
Roos, Holderness (plain exterior of NE building)
Collegiality ruined buildings at Tong, Shrops
String courses Sandiacre, Derbys
Acoustic virtues of wood Rattlesden, Suffolk
Acoustic jars Sandwich (St Clement), Kent
Organ lofts Cratfield, Suffolk (C15 organ loft now in W tower)
        & Diss, Norfolk (loft entry over vestry door, views from
        chancel and vestry)
Bellows lofts St Savin en Lavedan* (bellows from organ of
        *c*1580), & Strasbourg** (forge bellows), France
Organs and voices Alkerton, Oxon (pageant)
Large English organs St Brieuc, Brittany***
Size of bellows lofts Adderbury (large C19 reservoir) &
        Warmington, Oxon (C19 organ in chancel & wind-
        trunk of C19 organ from loft into organ) &
        Denningon, Suffolk (wind-trunk hole)
Size of organ lofts Hawstead, Suffolk

Introduction

LONG AGO, every Sunday the parish priest stood in the medieval pulpit and asked for prayers for all those 'that have honoured the church with light, lamp, vestment, or bell, or any ornaments by which the service of Almighty God is the better maintained and kept'.

It is very laudable to cultivate and perpetuate the memory of the past in this way, especially of people and their good deeds. But when these weekly bidding prayers fell silent, only the church buildings themselves remained; these instead became the memory banks of the communities that built and used them.

How to go about finding that capital invested in those banks, in order to borrow against it wisely in the future, is part of the aim of this book. It tries to distil some of the results of a ten-year investigation which started as research into the documents of the medieval church and then widened out into visiting, measuring and photographing over 800 medieval churches in England under the banner of 'Sounds Medieval: finding the sources of English music'. To help us carry out this research, The Society of Antiquaries of London very generously granted us three years' bursaries for expenses. Employing a unique and novel musical-archaeological approach to church buildings, our research tried to discover what physical infrastructures of medieval music still exist in churches throughout England, and in parts of Wales and Brittany.

The immediate reason for writing this short book, which has turned out to be a much longer essay than intended at first, has been the appearance of the long-awaited report of the Taylor Review of the Sustainability of English Churches and Cathedrals ('the Sustainability Review' for short). This was finally published on the 20th December 2017. Its chief recommendation is that networks of Community Support Advisors (CSAs) and Fabric Support Officers (FSOs) should be established. These officers are intended to help to maintain and widen the use of our heritage of around 8,300 Grade I and II* medieval churches despite the lowest-ever (and still declining) religious use of these buildings and considerable uncertainty over how they might continue to be sustained.

It is perhaps not surprising that a government report should recommend more 'officers', but if they are well chosen and trained, they could have a positive effect, though they will still need to be accompanied by well-trained experts in other fields such as archaeology, furnishings and fittings (including organs), landscape topography etc – and not least by those who have some insight into the medieval way of doing things, into the medieval mind.

Short-term memory and heritage-preservation can too often combine to give us the impression that what we see now is what was always there. But that is far from the case, as anyone who has worked in, used or even just visited churches over the past 60 years will know. If in the 1950s anyone had even dreamed of the idea that a medieval church might have a kitchen or toilets built into it, they would have been thought to be slightly 'odd' or even rather indecent. Yet these and the communal cup of coffee or tea after every service are now accepted as normal. So is an increasing use of town and a few country churches as places for cafés, banks, post offices, police stations and even shops. Churches no longer look the same, smell the same or are staffed, lighted or furnished in the same way as was 'normal' only a short life-time ago.

This increasing use of churches is definitely a good thing. Medieval churches were not built to become static and silent museum pieces ; they were designed as integrated functional spaces, totally suitable and appropriate for the uses they were put to when they were created. Sung offices and liturgies took up much of every day in every church, and until the 1530s churches were continually embellished and furnished. Around half the space in each church building was dedicated to daily musical ceremony while the other half was used by the people of the parish for their own ends, some overtly pious, others not. But the destruction of Latin books by order of Somerset, Cranmer and (nominally) Edward VI in 1548 put a sudden and violent end to music and former ceremonial practices, the chancels of English churches falling silent except for a five-year partial revival under Queen Mary. Their naves now became the undesigned places for community worship, using the new Common Prayer Books of 1549, 1552, 1559 and from 1662 onwards.

During the hundred years that followed the accession of Edward VI in early 1547, medieval church buildings were in an almost continual state of change to comply with orders from central government or local bishops. However, since 1660 English and Welsh churches have rarely been the objects of sweeping central ecclesiastical edicts and political or revolutionary interference, in sharp contrast with churches on the continent. This fact plus the general abandoning of their chancels until the mid C19 has meant that many more physical and discoverable signs of their former use are preserved in England and Wales than anywhere else in western Europe. It is still therefore uniquely possible to see why medieval churches were designed in the way they were, if we take the time to look.

What were the needs that inspired and directed the building of these churches up to possibly 900 years ago - about thirty-five memory-spans ? We should take some time to find out, because if we want to preserve a building and adapt it for new purposes it is wise to find out all we can about it and what it contains. It is equally important to appreciate what it no longer contains, because in every church many things that were there in 1530 are no longer there. But traces of them remain, and these traces need to be found, understood and preserved for future interpretation. If we do not find and understand these unique artefacts sheltered by every church, we risk destroying or degrading them. Especially if church buildings are going to become (again) in any real sense the focus of community activities – and this aim is woven into the texture of the Sustainability Review – we need to be aware that each and every stone, every piece of woodwork and glass has an historic community value : they are the capital in the parish's memory-banks.

That we need now more than ever before to understand our heritage of medieval churches is surely agreed by all who love and admire these wonderful buildings. But on the whole we do not understand them fully because they have been obscured by changes, myths and misconceptions. This long essay tries to use a new, previously almost unexplored, mix of music and social archaeology in an attempt to understand why churches were designed in the way they were, and the consequences that such an understanding might have for their future use.

The first thing to emphasise is that these churches were designed for multiple uses in a world in so many ways very different, especially in its aspirations and priorities, from anything we know today. But those glimpses of that world we can see in our churches will illuminate many otherwise puzzling and surprising aspects of these astonishing buildings. They are not just 'spiritual' places built for esoteric reasons, but were planned, designed, built and furnished for particular needs. Naturally, these needs were refined over the centuries, but we can still trace how they were reflected in the evolution of their design, starting in the Anglo-Saxon period and onward through the trauma of the Conquest to the eve of the equally traumatic Reformation.

Very few architects in the C19, and indeed C20, understood that medieval churches were functional buildings ; indeed, once these buildings had lost their original functions it was almost inevitable that the reasoned ways in which they were designed would be forgotten too. They therefore built new quasi-medieval churches in what might be described as 'fantasy mode' : buildings that looked medieval but were designed to be used in what were then contemporary C19 ways. When restoring their medieval buildings, they ran into the same problem, and by following counter-reformation models they used inappropriate examples.

To take just one example of the problem : archbishop William Laud, following continental counter-reformation practice caused by the demolition of rood screens all over continental Europe, decreed that altars should be railed off. For him this was for both practical and theological reasons, to protect what should be a set-apart space, though his puritanical contemporaries did not exactly see it like that. Most of what Laud did was quickly forgotten, but for some reason his altar rails never were, and their incorporation into 'restored' medieval chancels in places where floor levels had previously been deliberately disturbed by reformers caused not a few problems. Anyone can see the havoc these rails wrought in many chancels, made worse by being so often replaced by C19 factory-made fantasy-gothic designs for things which had never been found in medieval churches. They and their kneeling step were shoe-horned into chancels, often making a nonsense of the heights of floors at sedilias, piscinas, Easter sepulchres and the like.

The errors made during well-funded C19 restorations must alert us to what can happen if buildings are not understood. Demolishing, rebuilding, making new roofs, scraping, altering levels, putting in inappropriate stained glass, taking out screens, tiling floors in gothic-fantasy patterns and so on – we must not and I hope will not go any more along that road. Shouldn't we indeed reverse the most perverse of these 'restorations' to make better sense of our medieval chancels ?

This small book seeks to explain what is the essence of a fully-functioning medieval building. It cannot explain every single thing that can be found by careful search in every medieval church in Britain, but it can explain the basics. Every church was there to do the same job in its daily life, musically and socially. Each church followed much the same regulations and each church was provided with the same tools to carry out its work.

But there any unity stopped – each church also did these things in its own local way according to its own resources, material and intellectual, and did them at a faster or slower rate according to the wealth of its community. Even liturgical practices varied according to what regional 'Use' any particular church found itself attached. It was only with the legally-enforced intro-duction in 1549 of the first Prayer Book that uniformity of worship was achieved on a national scale.

Duties of people to their clerks

Early C14 ordinances of, among others, Bishop Quivil of Exeter and Archbishop Peckham of Canterbury set out those things that should be supplied by the people for the use of the clerks, thus :

> 'We will and ordain that the parishioners be bound to provide all the following : Legend, Antiphonal, Grayle, Psalter, Tropary, Ordinale, Missal, Manual, Chalice, the best Vestment with Chasuble, Dalmatic and Tunicle, and a Cope for the choir with all their belong-ings (that is, amice, girdle, maniple and stole, etc.) : the frontal for the High altar, with three cloths ; three

surplices ; a rochet ; the processional cross; a cross to carry to the sick ; a thurible ; a lantern ; a bell to ring when the Body of Christ is carried to the sick ; a pyx of ivory or silver for the Body of Christ ; the Lenten veil ; the Rogation Day banner ; the bells with their ropes ; a bier to carry the dead upon; the holy water vat ; the osculatorium for the Pax ; the paschal candlestick ; a font with its lock and key ; the images in the church ; the image of the patron saint in the chancel; the enclosure wall of the cemetery ; all repairs of the nave of the church, interior and exterior; repairs also in regard to the images of the crucifix and of the saints and to the glazed windows ; all repairs of books and vestments, when such restorations shall be necessary.'

Another Archbishop confirmed that 'all other repairs of the chancel and of other things not the object of special custom or agreement, pertain to the Rectors or Vicars'.

ABC of a medieval church

IT IS VITAL to understand that a medieval church was a building which was deliberately divided up into two major parts, each with its own purpose.

The word 'church' in ME (Medieval, or if you prefer, Middle English) did not mean the whole building but a specific part of it. Modern parishes still have 'church wardens', and in these words lies the fossil-relic of a usage that was quite specific until the Reformation. They were people (nearly always male) who were usually elected annually by the lay folk of the parish to look after their part of the building, the centre of their communal life. 'Their part' lay west of the screen or screens that separated it from the part which contained what in ME were called the 'altars' : the sanctuary, the various eastern chapels and their ancillary buildings lying east of the screens. The peoples' part, for which their wardens were reponsible was called 'the church' , or in Latin *eccelsia*. That is why those people who into whose care the goods of the people and their part of building were

confided were called 'church wardens', the guardians of
the church who were called to account for their
stewardship of the church's goods when their period of
office came to an end. These accounts (CWA) also served
as the basis for the Sunday bede prayer and for a special
annual day of commemoration of donors to the church.
The set of CWA from Great Dunmow in Essex is still
contained in a leather cover embossed with 'Jesu, Mary,
pray for the souls of those mentioned herein'.

The peoples' western part of the church building
comprised what we now call the nave and its aisles. It
included also the two porches to north and south and the
tower to the west, and all that was kept in these. This
meant not only bells but sometimes also the goods for
which the wardens were responsible.

A short glossary

Before going any further, though, a basic vocabulary is
needed because, as we have just seen, ME words do not
necessarily mean or imply what we think they do now.
Confusingly too, many words were brought into use in
the C17 and later to describe features in church whose
original use had already been discontinued and therefore
at least partly forgotten.

Aisle – this is modern English (first used about 1731,
from the French for 'wing', apparently), substituted for
the ME and modern word 'alley' which was used to refer
to the middle part of the peoples' *ecclesia* as well as its
north or south side areas. These alleys were marked by a
general absence of what we now call 'pews' ; even when
they do start to make an appearance in the late C15,
benches or forms were restricted to the edges of the
north and south alleys. Alleys were wide processional
paths, including the central one, recalled still in folk
memory as the one along which couples walk 'up the
aisle' at weddings. If there were stone seats, these were
there at least partly to be used by people waiting for
something, or resting, as is indicated by the placing of
such seats on pilgrimage paths along alleys in churches

and cathedrals which lead towards shrines. Though there is little indication of loose benches or stools in CWA or inventories, the likely presence of these in the *ecclesia* is suggested by their documented presence in chancels – see 'sedilia' below.

Altar – the word used in ME for what we now tend to call a chapel inside a church building. So, for instance, references were made to 'a Lady altar' rather than to 'a Lady chapel'.

Chancel – this word in English is not derived from 'cancelli' (Italian for a side-gate or grille) as is often supposed, but from the place where music was sung or chanted. It is a fairly late comer to ME documents, but when it does finally surface in late C15 CWA (as at Bishop's Stortford in Hertfordshire) it is spelt 'chaunsell'. This seems to be appropriate for the part of the church (comprising the quire to its west and the sanctuary to the east) where services were always chanted.

Nave – in ME documents, this word (always in Latin, *navis*) seems to be restricted to the western parts of monastery churches. Monastic naves were not available to lay people but were used for processions, with marked-out paths ; these naves also included additional altars under its arches. In ME the nave of a parish church was, as we have seen, called 'the church' or, in Latin, *ecclesia*.

Sanctuary – the eastern part of the chancel beyond the line between the chancel's entry door from the outside and the vestry door opposite to it.

Screen – an omnibus word for all the types of enclosures to be found in a church building. It might refer to the main rood screen and its platform, balustrades etc as a whole, usually fixed at the east end of the *ecclesia*, or to a quire screen at the west end of the quire (especially if there was an intervening tower space in a cruciform church building), or to any side screens set up between quire and chancel side altars, or between altars in transepts or around altars set up in the *ecclesia*.

Transept – a word first found in use in 1538, according to the Shorter Oxford Dictionary. Since transepts were built to house lateral chapels (and incidentally also to support any central tower), probably they would have originally been spoken of as places for 'side' or (by contrast with the main one) 'low' altars, or would be even more likely to be described by their dedicated name, such as 'Lady altar' or 'St Giles' guild altar'.

Outside the church building

It is always a good idea to walk round the outside of a church before going into it, as John Betjeman reminded us. Walk round it clockwise, not widdershins ! One might see things there that cannot be seen from the inside, such as sanctus bell turrets, usually though not always on the east gable of the nave roof, upper rooms ('lofts' in ME) over porches, the upper parts of towers, buildings on the north side of the chancel or aisles, and sometimes some evidence of missing NE and E sacristies or other parts of the church building. Most histories of churches do not concern themselves enough with what surrounded the church : the churchyard and its cross, and the buildings that bordered it. Nor do we hear much about where the parish's wayside, cross-roads and boundary crosses, chapels and church houses were sited. The housing of priests and auxiliary staff needs to be described, too.

Back in the yard, it is worth looking to see what remains of any plants – especially the very slow-growing box, which was used, with willow, yew and rosemary on Palm Sunday - or for any signs of plants that could be used to fumigate or scent the church, or of rushes to be spread on its floors. Many references in CWA to paths being scoured and kept free of ordure suggest that perhaps the church flock of sheep was kept in the yard, too ; sheep are still used for instance on the Romney Marsh to keep church yard grass down, but no church there has its own flock these days. The presence of yew trees in church yards is obvious and often commented upon ; they can be much older than the church building, and are therefore likely to be signs of a pre-Christian site that the church has taken over. They were not, apparently, used for making bows, for which –ironically – French yew was superior.

Church yards were constantly re-used, their soil turned over time and again for burials. At four feet down for an adult and two for a child, with their bodies wrapped in shrouds not coffins, grave pits did not need to be as large as most are now. Nor therefore did the yards, and their original boundaries (which may have included some housing now disappeared) will have become obscured. Some now lonely churches may have had villages around them that for some reason have disappeared too (as at Ab Kettleby and Sproxton in Leicestershire) ; almost all medieval clergy housing has gone too, giving the impression perhaps that there was none, or that there was no local priest or any other staff. The fact that there is now rarely any visible presence of clergy in their parishes or in their churches outside services does not remotely reflect what we know from documentary sources to have been the norm in medieval practice – indeed, it does not reflect the best practice of only 60 years ago.

Look at the topography of the church yard, its trees (any box or willows ?) ; were there any local wells (springs) or rivers ? Consider why the church is where it is in relation to the village/town/manor. Imagine the church building as it was, with a coat of lime-washed plaster on the outside, with no gutters or down-pipes ; wonder if there were 'eaves-drip burials' or burials in or near porches, and where they might have been ? Do the down-pipes now cut through 'string courses' ? Look at roof-line changes and evidence of building changes right through to C19 alterations – how do these changes relate to changes from thatched to tiled roofs and possibly to C19 slates now ? Are windows still barred ? If so, which are barred, and why ? What does this barring tell us about the wealth of the church it was designed to protect ; which part of the church contained that wealth ? If barred windows are to be found only in windows in the chancel, how was this area secured from access from inside the church ?

What sort of church was it ? Was it a parish church or just a chapel ? Does the example of Morebath in Devon, well-known from Eamon Duffy's reworking of its CWA, show that there were no 'poor' churches ? Did they become poor later, with signs of retrenchment, and if so why ? Where did the church's money come from originally and where did it go to later ? How can their financial history still be honestly expressed, transmitted and understood ?

Look at old maps to see if there are fields associated with the church, such as chantry fields ; see if there are extant CWA or articles in local county archaeological and historical journals ; look at the list of rectors or vicars and try to work out who really was in control of the churches (or more likely their chancels) at any given time ; try to find records of what the church was like in the early C19, and then compare them with what happened during C19 restorations : what was found, what was removed or re-hidden.

This information provides the background to our understanding how the church functioned as a community asset, from birth to death – and afterwards.

A is for Altars

THE EASTERN PART of almost every church building is at the same time the most and the least altered part of the church. Former north-western Roman churches on the continent were either severely emptied to fit them for Calvinistic word-based (preaching) services, or altered in various ways by different Lutheran confessions or, as mentioned above, radically altered by the Roman Tridentine counter-reformation. By contrast, the chancels of churches taken over by the new Church of England (and Wales) were more gradually emptied of most of their ornaments in a long series of government-directed purges, the whole process taking 70 years to roll through the C16. Although these changes deprived chancels of an astonishing amount of material (ornaments certainly, but also actual buildings, as we will see), they did not always involve the sort of wholesale gutting seen elsewhere in Europe. Many features were not destroyed outright but covered up ('defaced' can and did mean hiding an object, not only spoiling it), only to be rediscovered and not always well understood in the restoration boom-years of the 1850s and 60s, and later.

This work was done often under the impulse and aegis of the Camden Society, unfortunately before later C19 scholarship might have interpreted and mitigated what was done. The model for these restorations was a watered-down version of continental changes made as a result of the Council of Trent ; not an appropriate model. But on the whole, in England sufficient vestiges remain for us to recreate at least in imagination (or virtually) the medieval chancel as it really was.

So let us have a close look at a parish church's chancel as it was designed, or re-designed, to function until the death of Henry VIII in January 1547. What follows has to be a generalised description. It cannot attempt to describe every local or historical variant but tries to explain why certain features were there and what we might still be able to discover. We will start at the west end of the chancel, looking eastwards from where the rood screen stands or stood, under the chancel arch.

Quire stalls

Usually a single step led up into the chancel from the
nave, the rood screen's sole plate being laid on this step.
To our right (south) and left (north) as we move
eastwards are the quire stalls. Their back rows follow the
north and south walls and then turn through ninety
degrees along the east edge of the chancel arch
abutments and the base of the rood-screen. Even if these
stalls perished a long time ago while the chancel was
abandoned, there may still be signs in the walls, and
especially in the NW and SW corners, of fixings or
stonework that has been cut out to accommodate these
stalls, about 36 to 40 inches up from the floor. Notice
too that often windows are lower at the chancel's west
end than elsewhere, in order to let more light in at dawn
onto the desks of the stalls here from which the daily
early morning offices of Matins and Lauds would be
sung. Some windows here might also have been
extended downwards to enhance this lighting (and then
blocked up later) ; in rare places there are still signs of
hinges for the shutters on these windows.

The back-row stalls are set on a plinth, with at least one
step up into them. They may have individual 'misericord' seats or may be benches, and were occupied by
senior parochial clergy, the priests and deacons, together
with the older lay singers and senior clerks such as the

holy-water clerks. These last worked in the sanctuary at
mass time but were expected also to attend at least the
two primary daily offices of matins and vespers. The
back row stalls would also be used by visiting clergy of
rank but the idea that misericord stalls in parish
churches were made for monks cannot be correct, since
the essence of a cloistered life is that a fully-professed
monk never leaves his convent or monastery. However,
the senior officers of a monastery, if it was the rector of a
particular church and held its advowson, might well
attend important events in parochial life such as patronal
festivals, episcopal or archidiaconal visitations or the
installation of a new vicar nominated by them. It was
anyway the rector's responsibility to provide these quire
stalls as well as all the rest of the chancel's furnishings.

An essential distinction was made between the quire
stalls and seats elsewhere. The clue is in their names :
just as horses usually stand in their stalls in stables,
quire stalls are designed for standing (to sing) in – or,
since they are capacious, for kneeling. Apart from
lessons (chosen extracts from the bible) which were
spoken, almost the whole of the offices were sung, as was
about two-thirds of a medieval mass. The remaining

third of a mass consisted of a short homily (if there was one) and the epistle (at which one sat) and the 'silent' (spoken or sung in a 'low' voice) consecration canon. The eloquence of this near-silence, wrapped around with so much music, has to be experienced to be appreciated.

A lower and narrower set of stalls, not always with 'returned' seats and desks because many chancels are too narrow to allow room for these, was occupied by less senior clerks such as adolescent singers, epistolers, acolytes and candle carriers. Young singers and those still learning the essentials – the whole psalter and much else besides, all by heart – before being allowed to enter the quire stalls sat on loose benches placed on the floor in front of this lower row. Since ME for bench is 'form', these young boys, from the age of six upwards, therefore started their singing career on 'the first form', the phrase used until quite recently to describe the entry class in state schools. Such benches could be cleared away when not needed (boys were not expected to attend minor offices) or when the singers were grouped around a large 'desk' or lectern, placed when needed in the centre of the quire between the fixed stalls, in order to sing complex written music.

These quire stalls therefore demonstrate in visual terms the choir's hierarchy. A boy admitted solemnly into the choir would receive a tonsure like all his fellow clerks and be expected gradually to rise through the rows of stalls. In almost every church he would be taught the rudiments and then encouraged to master increasingly complex musical tasks including learning to play the organ if there was one. Such teaching was usually part of the job description of a chantry priest. It would not stop when a boy's voice broke, nor would he leave off singing in the choir. But he would progress to be taught to write Latin (it would be inevitable that he could read it by then) and the basics of rhetoric. If he showed promise, he might be given a bursary to enter either a local college or one of the Oxbridge halls. At the age of 18 he would need to decide whether to go forward for ordination to higher clerical ranks or to remain a lay person, perhaps taking a post as a lay vicar choral (substituting for canons in a college or cathedral), and thus aiming to pursue a professional career in music.

Either way, this system, at whatever level it was pursued, produced experienced lay singers and organ players and – crucially – also a priesthood that was thoroughly trained in the practice of music. No senior priest, be he monastic or secular, would have been promoted without the essential qualification of being thoroughly competent to lead the singing at all the complex services of the church. It does not take much imagination to understand what a profoundly different approach a professionally-trained musician-priest would bring to the preparation and performance of services.

The chancel door

Quire stalls usually extended all the way eastwards to the next step in the chancel. This second step was set across the chancel, just westwards of the outside doorway into it. All who worked in the chancel and sanctuary arrived through this door, the rood or quire screen gates or doors being locked except to allow processions to enter the quire from the nave. Usually opposite that entry doorway (unless for some special reason it was not on the south side of the church) was the internal door to the vestry block that stood to the north of the sanctuary. Between these two doors was a level space delineated by the step up from between the quire stalls to its west and a third step up into the sanctuary on its eastern edge. We do not know what this area was called in parish churches, but similar spaces in collegiate churches were called 'gradus' or 'levels'. The whole chancel was graded, rising from west to east as the altar was approached, a visual echo of the psalms of ascent to Jerusalem often sung as a group in offices on special feast days.

It is very rare for there not to be a chancel door, its absence normally being due to a post-medieval shortening of the chancel. The doorway is usually between six and seven feet in height, with a higher inner lobby within the thickness of the wall, into which the door opens. This inner part, being almost always higher than is needed for the door to turn into, needs some explanation, but I have neither seen, nor can think of, anything convincing in this respect. If the doorway sill is not at the same height as the 'gradus' it opens into, there has usually been some C19 or earlier alteration of levels, and this needs to be explained case by individual case. Outside, later drains or a gradual raising of the yard by burials (or spoil from the foundations of, for instance, added chancel aisles), will mean a change in levels here too, as one can assume that when the doorway was made it opened both ways onto areas level with it and without any need for steps.

Seats for mass celebrants

Apart from the altar, the most prominent furnishings (in side or low chapels as well as near the high altar) might be the seats for the clergy officiating in the sanctuary at mass-time, in the C19 called 'sedilia'. There were usually three of these, nearly always placed on the south side of the sanctuary and usually fitted into the dropped sill of a window west of a 'piscina'. The seats might have been wooden, in which case they did not survive the C17, or in stone, often with elaborate carved surroundings. Here the three mass celebrants could sit on cushions (in order of precedence, the most senior on a higher seat-ledge furthest to the east) at times when they were not themselves singing or speaking, as during the epistle and gradual or during a homily.

Sculptures around and above the three seats are often interesting, not only for their complexity but for their subjects. These might include cheeky animals or even leering faces, perhaps as reminders of the ever-present temptation of the more senior clergy to become proud or unsociable. Many of these sets of seats would have been cut back and plastered over in the later C16, or even destroyed altogether, leaving only a higher outside window sill here as witness. Many of these sculptures were also heavily restored and scraped in the C19, but if they escaped serious damage, perhaps by being hidden under plaster, they might still have traces of their original colours. So very few of these have their original colouring restored that the greatest care needs to be taken. At Lawford in Essex, for example, there are elaborate sedilia canopies and other carvings including an amazing series of players and acrobats climbing round a chancel window. They are still covered thickly in layers of whitewash, leaving one to wonder what colours might lie beneath this white crust.

Not all the many furnishings a medieval chancel might contain were sought for during the C19, so some still lie under plaster. The received wisdom in the C19 and later was that the Reformation was so popular that people were glad to see such things disappear. On the contrary, at least some of these were paid for by the church folk, especially such items as piscina and sedilia near their guild altars. Recent documentary research though confirms what one should have suspected : that if people thought they could get away with preserving something precious (despite the terrible threats often made to dissuade them) they did so, either by removing them or hiding them in plain sight under plaster – as they were evidently also to do in the C17 when faced with the removal of such precious things as fonts or the 'defacing' of carvings on them.

Lighting the sanctuary

Windows in the sanctuary, like those in the quire, were made larger towards the end of the medieval period to bring more light to this area. This was partly done to show off the increasingly elaborate furnishings there but also to light new desks for the singing of the epistle and gospel – and the 'last gospel' which concluded mass, too. This evolution can still be traced now, because even where the whole building fabric itself has not been rebuilt with large windows on three sides of the

sanctuary, larger windows will have been inserted, particularly on its south side. Looking carefully and quizzically at the fenestration of chancels - why are the windows placed where they are ? – is arguably more useful as well as more interesting than describing them only by their typology (lancet, decorated, perpendicular etc). If visitors are encouraged to ask such questions, they will gain much from the exercise ; indeed, scholars too might be able to date windows more closely by doing this. The long period from the 1360s onwards, currently lumped together under 'perpendicular' because it has not been possible to date such windows accurately based only on their tracery styles, needs to be teased apart. Finding practical reasons for these windows might be a start.

It is also potentially more fascinating for the average visitor to be invited to explore such ideas, or to consider *why* visible features are there, rather than to be told *what* he or she can see perfectly well for him or herself, but the latter approach is all too often the staple diet of church history-guides. In an interactive world, an 'innocent' enquiring visitor might anyway be able to suggest a fruitful or more compelling explanation for, or question about, such features.

Lavabos

Moving further eastwards, another vital item for the performance of the mass is a 'piscina', one of the C19 names (others included 'lavatorium') for the low niche in usually a south but sometimes an east wall near every altar. The hole in the base of the piscina allowed water to run away to ground at the end of mass when the chalice and paten, with any remains of consecrated elements, were washed, but this niche had other functions as well. It contained a shelf used to house the chalice when this was brought in by a deacon at the start of mass, hence its common trefoiled form. Before mass, a junior clerk would also place small glass or pewter cruets containing water and wine there, so the niche also includes space for these either on that shelf, or in a space next to the drain, which is set off-centre for this purpose or given a wide surround. The height available above the centre of the shelf, into the head of the trefoil, might give us a useful clue as to the size of medieval chalices, all then-surviving examples of which (apart from those buried with prelates) were called in for destruction in the 1570s. Using the water from a cruet, poured by a server, the priest also washed his hands here at the start of the canon of the mass while saying in a low voice 'Lavabo inter innocentes manus meas et circumdabo altare tuum, Domine', so it is possible that its ME name was a 'lavabo'. However, some vestries were also provided with piscinas, presumably for ritual hand-washing before mass and to clean more thoroughly the vessels brought back to them afterwards.

Stobbes

Another essential item that needed to be near an altar was an 'aumbry' (yet again a modern word), a cupboard set into a wall, one ME description of which was 'a stobbe'. These contained altar books and were often lockable, which if so suggests that these stobbes were also their usual storage place. Most churches possessed far more than the dozen or so books they were obliged to have and keep in good repair. Some had so many that unless further cupboards are yet to be found hidden in walls it is hard to see where all of these might have been kept. However, the internal dimensions of these cupboards, and any shelves, can (as with chalices in piscinas) be taken to indicate the size of the various larger 'volumes' and smaller 'books' that were in use

upon altars, laid there on cushions or small desks, or placed on epistle or gospel desks. Some of these stobbes are quite deep and even go round corners, as if to hide small items from view, perhaps smaller books or ornaments. Similar cupboards are also occasionally found near quire stalls and again they might give us some indication of the size of books used there.

Easter sepulchres

Usually opposite the 'sedilia' was the Easter sepulchre. This was a permanent or temporary structure, usually on the north side of the sanctuary. If temporary, it was set up for use during the ceremonies of the second part of Holy Week, the week before Easter Day, and then removed. No known complete example of these temporary structures survives. Permanent sepulchres comprise either a specially-designed carved (and coloured) stone structure with a recess which in some examples includes a concealed access to earth placed in the thickness of the wall below it. They also have or had painted designs on their back walls and their decoration included carvings of angels, disciples and sleeping soldiers. Some tombs were also specially designed, in this place of honour, to double as Easter sepulchres. They included some of their characteristic features, so often including quarter-foils in their bases as to make one wonder if these had a special significance.

Squints

This is a general name for various horizontal square or rectangular holes through walls, occasionally even through the backs of Easter sepulchres. In general they tend to be oriented towards the east and often the high altar. Larger ones might be there so that the faithful, grouped beyond the rood screen, are able to see a particular altar. Other squints are there so that a priest at a side altar, or in a chantry, might be able to delay the moment of his elevation of the host at consecration, so respecting the primacy of the elevation at the high altar. Such squints need to be examined from both ends using two people, moving until both are in full view. This will help establish just where low altars were actually placed, since all side altars in churches are relatively-recent restorations and not necessarily placed exactly where their medieval predecessors were.

Squints were also used by those who rang bells in turrets or towers at the elevation so that people at home or in the fields or workshops could acknowledge the moment of consecration. Since the canon of the mass is said in a low voice, it was necessary for the ringer to see the elevation. Small bells were rung at this point by those near enough to the altar to hear what was going on, and a tower or turret ringer could pick up from this, but the fact that there is a way of seeing as well as (possibly) hearing suggests that perhaps it was intended that these bells should be rung simultaneously. Many western towers also have openings on their east faces that give directly on to the high altar for the same reason. Upper bellows rooms behind organs also have small windows, high on the north side of chancels, so that bellows operators know it is time to start work when singers stand and get ready to sing. These squint-window-tunnels might have been blocked when a two-storey vestry was demolished or turned into a single-storey one. At Castle Acre parish church in Norfolk, whoever blocked it seems to have had the ghoulish idea of putting a couple of skulls and some femur bones into its passage. The vicar there assured us that these relics had a real value still, as warnings for any misbehaving choir-children.

Tabernacles

In especially-honoured positions on each side of the east window, statues of the church's patron and often Our Lady were placed upon corbels or within more complex 'tabernacles'. Although this word is now used to describe a lockable place for consecrated hosts above and behind a counter-reformation altar, in ME churches it was the name for a niche to shelter a wooden or stone statue.

Pyxes

Suspended above the front of the altar was a pyx, a silver or ivory box containing a consecrated host and covered by a finely-embroidered cloth. It was held up by a rope or chain which ran over a pulley on a beam or in the ceiling or celure, allowing it to be lowered. Signs of this system (pulleys, or hooks to belay the cord) are rare but any small iron fixtures of this sort – including hooks for war-time blackout curtains – need to be interpreted and preserved scrupulously. Painting over 'untidy marks' or replastering any wall surfaces before exploring them carefully is false tidiness, the enemy of conservation.

Veils

The practice of veiling statues in Lent was re-introduced in the C20, but in medieval period veiling included the practice of obscuring the altar as well during Lent. The priest was also veiled during the canon of the mass, the elevation of the host above the veil being what people who were gathered in their church had come to witness. Very few signs remain of these veils. The rather enigmatic remains at Postling in Kent (two pairs of sawn-off beam ends in the sanctuary) might once have been beams for supporting rope-pulleys with which to raise and lower such a veil, as would the remains of a similarly-placed beam (now seeming far too low because of a C19 raising of the sanctuary floor level) at Clare in Suffolk.

Tiles

Church historians need to be aware that a tiler was not only concerned with making and laying floor tiles but also with what in ME are called 'wall tiles' : bricks in modern English. We now see so many tiles in chancels rebuilt in the C19 that we might assume them to be more common than perhaps they were. C19 examples are anyway not always coloured naturally (green and mauve tiles are especially out of place), and are glazed with a sort of dead-alive uniformity. Medieval floor tiles, which seem to be confined with very few exceptions to chancels and areas round altars, clearly would have had an enriching effect on sunlight falling on them through southern windows but they may have had a more practical function as well. At Salle in Norfolk, it seems likely that the various patterns of the tiling between the quire stalls and in the sanctuary have some

ritual significance. But what this may have been is not
the only secret this great church has yet to divulge.

Retables and mensa slabs

If people are surprised about the presence of organs in
medieval chancels, they would be even more surprised to
know that another entire species of English art was once
there too. With only four fairly-complete examples of
wooden English retables, there are indeed far fewer

traces of retables in English churches than traces of organs. One of these retables is now in a small country church thanks to its fortunate and incidental purchase in 1778 from a house in Stradbroke in Suffolk by Lord Henniker, a local land-owner. He then promptly had it stored in a barn from where it was not to be rescued by a descendant until 1927 who placed it in a local church. It was finally identified, conserved, cleaned and properly displayed in recent times. This is a Dominican retable, probably painted in a Norwich workshop c1330 for Thetford priory, and now in Thornham Parva church in Suffolk. The other examples are in Norwich cathedral, Westminster Abbey and the British Museum (from Kingston Lacey in Dorset).

But CWA are full of references to 'tables' : either to their purchase or in inventories, where they are sometimes described as being made of alabaster. They consisted of coloured scenes from the life of Jesus or his mother or other saints and were coloured and set up behind or next to altars. Marks on the walls near altars in the 'nine altars' eastern extension of Fountains Abbey, for example, must have been where these were fixed ; at Rievaulx and elsewhere, fragments of tables were found in the ground near where nave altars had been, no doubt falling there when altars were demolished along with the rest of the fittings at the destruction of the monasteries. When altars in parish churches and chapels were ordered to be taken down by Edward VI, the destruction of these inevitably involved removal of their tables as well. This was because altars consisted of large slabs of stone which were set into the east wall of the sanctuary, their fronts being supported either on a plinth of stones or two pillars. Pictorial alabaster and wooden tables were set on top of and behind these mensa slabs in a row or rows between them and the sill of the east window.

Another style of retable was a taller, carved stone frame for tables and statues set up at the east end of the sanctuary in the absence of a window there, or covering it. Traces of these can be found in a number of places, either dreadfully degraded and almost unrecogniseable, as in the N choir aisle of the former abbey (now cathedral) at Bristol, or in a better state in the E aisle of the S transept above the Lady altar at Patrington in Holderness.

An almost-complete tall stone retable was found about 70 years ago in Audignon church in the Landes in southern France, preserved by having been hidden behind a tall wooden C17 counter-reformation 'reredos' of the type familiar to visitors to French churches (see colour plate). It can be dated to the early C15 by reference to the clothing style of the people portrayed on it, and is called locally 'the English retable'. This description comes about partly because this southern-Acquitaine region was (to put it mildly) under the influence of the English for a long period, and it seems to have been assumed that the work was made by English craftsmen. Groups of travelling craftsmen, natives of all countries, are indeed known to have worked everywhere in NW Europe. Contacts made through the large Benedictine abbey at St Sever nearby might have been a reason for their working in the romanesque church of Audignon, which also lies on one of the Compostella routes.

When the retable was set up it created a wall of stone across the apse, the space behind becoming a sacristy entered by a doorway through the south side of the retable wall. It is still a large structure, consisting of three superimposed rows of tabernacles, their vertical dividers rising originally to pinnacles. Each niche consists of a painted scene from the life of Jesus and of saints and doctors (theologians). A crucifixion scene is painted in the centre, which suggests that there a separate crucifix was not placed on the mensa. The mensa slab of Audignon's high altar was carried by this wall too – its width can still be seen – and one can see all too easily how a less substantial retable structure would have been brought down if a mensa was removed.

Traces of the width of mensa slabs can still be seen in unevenness, disturbance or infilling in the east walls in some English churches, but signs of complete English wall-retables of the Audignon type (if this was indeed a style also practised widely in England) are very difficult to find. Tall 'reredoses' that cover the east walls of the former chantry chapels of, for example, New College or All Souls' colleges in Oxford are however larger (and now colourless) versions of it. The parish church of Hitchin in Hertfordshire has the footings of a wall between the sanctuary and a retro-quire which might have supported such a structure. There are also a few places where retables might yet be found but they, like other hidden items, await investigation with wall-reading radar.

If retables such as Audignon's – or smaller versions that fitted under east windows - were at all common in England, their loss is truly lamentable. All we have now are some alabaster relics removed from their designed context, their original impact and purpose totally lost.

There are quite a few examples of mensas around, either still in floors or taken up again, placed on stone supports and used once again as altar slabs. It is one of mysteries of the Reformation how these, marked with five crosses and solemnly consecrated with hallowed oils, could have been made targets for supposedly religious reasons. Mensas being foci of the 'idolatry of transubstantiation' seems to have been the chief motive for forcing parishes to take them down with any retables and deliberately defile them by placing them underfoot.

Brass and brasses

The same misplaced zeal also saw the continual ripping up of brasses from monuments, at first for ideological reasons, saying that they held 'superstitious' texts, and then just so as to sell the brass as scap metal. Edward VI had inherited completely empty royal coffers from his father (who had himself inherited the fullest treasury in Europe), so in the years around 1550 the seizure of anything saleable in churches became institutionalised. Among things sold were many candlesticks and what had previously been described in inventories as 'great eagle desks'. These had been made in East Anglian workshops, using traded Flemish 'latten', an expensive and difficult to produce brass-like alloy of copper, zinc and lead, each bird being assembled from around 24 cast parts. They were placed in the sanctuary as lecterns to hold large and heavy wood-bound gospel books. Victorian near-copies now hold bibles in naves (when not relegated to the side-lines) but it is possible quite easily to tell which is which, if there is any doubt. Look at their wings ; in medieval ones their flight feathers curve outwards to hold wide 'gospellers', but C19 bible-eagles have their wings curving inwards.

Survival stories of these eagles, including their being hidden in ponds, need to be told as dreadful warnings, highly indicative of terrible times in which misplaced zeal was allowed to lead to orgies of destruction. We might think we do better than that now, but I have seen – and opposed – C21 faculties seeking permission to dispose of crucifixes, candlesticks and organs, all items which had previously been targetted in the C16. This suggests that we have not quite grown out of the idea that what we may not like or appreciate now can be got rid of : another form of defacing, or removing from memory.

All other portable altar equipment – their small desks, larger candlesticks, crucifixes and the tall free-standing candelabra – and such items as the processional crosses (often made using valuable metals and gems) were also sold off in the C16, leaving most churches with a chalice and a few vestments. Almost all bells would have disappeared from towers too but Edward's early death stopped this except in easily-accessible towers such as those in coastal or port towns where they were taken out, weighed and exported. Finally, any surviving medieval chalices were called in under Elizabeth I in the 1570s and melted down, churches being paid a few pounds if they could not afford to replace them with new ones.

NORTH-EAST BUILDINGS : THE SERVICE BLOCK

Associated with those parts of the chancels we can still see – the central quire or choir and the chancel aisles with their present or former altars – were other buildings which in many cases do not survive or were radically replaced in the C19.

As a result of the considerable late-medieval stock of ornaments, vestments and music books being dispersed – sold or burned - from 1547 onwards, there was no longer any use for the former sacristies and treasuries that would have contained all these. These were the goods of the whole church, those items recorded in CWA and commemorated in the reading of bede-rolls. Church wardens, whose remit previously would not have run beyond the rood screen, already had their storage places in lofts over porches, in towers and church houses. The minimal furnishings left by Edward's commissioners for the occasional celebration of Communion services in the chancel (a chalice and paten, one set of vestments, later reduced to a surplice, and two candle-sticks) would not exactly have taken up much space. So a large number of buildings on the north side of the church that had been directly accessible from the chancel were allowed to fall into disrepair.

This process was accelerated by the financial pressures that had started with devaluations of the currency under Henry VIII in the 1540s and then repeated by his successors, creating continual monetary inflation throughout the rest of the C16. Totally new civic rather than religious duties were imposed on wardens during that time too : raising or 'gathering' church rates (a new tax, not needed before), newly-required provisions for dealing with the newly-created classes of poor, infirm and vagrants, or the support of soldiers, and even storage of their weapons and armour.

These meant that the upkeep of churches became a matter of deciding on priorities. Maintaining a now-useless building at the opposite end of the church from where the parishioners gathered would not have been a high priority. Even chancels themselves were allowed by their absent rectors to fall down wholly or partially. This happened especially frequently in rural Lincolnshire, right up to the mid-C19, where in some places previously essential items such as the sedilia and piscina are still absent, their chancels never having been rebuilt to their original proportions.

There are significant clues as to the previous existence of these NE buildings. Opposite the (usually) southern door which gives entry from the outside into the chancel is another doorway in the chancel's north wall. If this doorway is plainly medieval in style, it would have led into a number of possibly-related buildings not confined to being the simple vestries they were usually 'restored' or rebuilt into in the C19. They might have been a complex mixture of storage areas, vesting rooms, strong-rooms and places for the bellows of an organ. Some were in addition (or instead) small chantries – an altar in a separate room equipped like a miniature chancel chapel. It is quite difficult to make hard and fast rules about what might have lain beyond these NE 'vestry' doors, and therefore it is all the more important that any clues should not be obscured or even removed now, either inside the chancel or outside it.

Beyond that door there might have been a simple one-room vestry where all the vestments, ornaments and books of the quire and sanctuary were kept safely. A larger, collegiate, church would require much more space as time went on, and there are places where such larger accommodation was bolted on to an existing fabric. A completely-rebuilt late medieval chancel will have been provided with extensive vestries, sacristies and treasuries; those at St Peter Mancroft in Norwich, for instance, were arranged on two floors. For security reasons, such vestries did not usually have outside doors or large windows, and those windows they did have would have been secured with strong wrought-iron bars that are still often in place.

By contrast, a chantry on this site would be differently designed. It would need to be well lit, being on the north and not having direct sunlight, so an east window and a largish one to the north would be desirable. The other main signs of a chantry might be the remains of an 'altar pace', the raised area round and under the position of the altar, and a piscina usually in the south wall and perhaps signs of a retable or statue niche. There might be a more ornamental ceiling than would be usual for a vestry, and signs of frescoes. Normally there would be an original (medieval) outer door so that the chantry priest could come to his altar without having to traverse the main sanctuary to go to sing his masses. There is very often a squint between the chantry and the main altar ; sometimes this is covered by a shutter and occasionally partly concealed by going through the corner of a fixed Easter sepulchre or tomb-sepulchre.

It is often clear from the too rarely-visited outside NE corner of the chancel, that a substantial building here has been allowed to fall down. Corbels which supported a cross-beam on which rafters were laid to form a cat-slide roof can often be seen, often placed so high as to make the previous existence of a two-storey building here really certain. The ground-area dimensions of this building and any entry doors to it are often now almost impossible to ascertain, though the absence of graves in this area might be indicative ; there are sometimes also some remnants of foundations. If this building survived (even as a ruin) until the end of the C18, it is possible that a local artist or an antiquarian county historian might have visited the church and made a sketch or water colour of it from this angle, though this is not a commonly painted or drawn view unless it is very obvious from the nearest main road. (Views taken from the south-west are generally much more popular, especially when they can include an ornate south porch.) Other views of the church from various dates displayed in churches (often in vestries) are also well worth checking. Quite a number of these disappeared buildings have piscinas or the remnants of them on their outsides ; some even have what appear to be the backs of Easter Sepulchres or of the squints that pierced this wall.

NOSELEY.N.W

Rather surprisingly, there are also complete and very
substantial buildings that are still attached to or even
built into churches which have not been interpreted.
These are almost always two-storey buildings with upper
windows and are as high as their contiguous chancels or
aisles. They might lack for instance their internal
(upper) floor(s), and in such cases sometimes the
staircases that led up to the upper floor have gone as
well. Often C19 external doorways have been punched
through the original fabric. Conversion or 'restoration'
of their ground floors into vestries might also have
eradicated or covered previous evidence of use, causing
interpretation difficulties which are accentuated by the
intrusive introduction of C19 fireplaces and C21
cupboards and filing cabinets. However, such churches
might also have archives (CWA or inventories) that show
what goods were stored in the eastern areas, and these
can give us good clues as to the extent of storage that was
necessary.

We might understand the use of the ground floor as a
vestry or sacristy or even chantry, but what was the
upper room for ? If you believe too many church guides,

here lived the priest, or perhaps an anchorite, or perhaps the sacrist or sexton. Such 'explanations' are often preceded by that tell-tale phrase, 'without doubt'. But again, if you consider the large quantity and high value of possessions of what now appear to be quite 'ordinary' churches as shown in their ME inventories, it becomes clear that these higher buildings, protected first by the door into the chancel, then by doors at the foot and top of their staircases, and often with still-existing shutters and barred windows, were designed as safe storage places or treasuries. They may also have had another purpose, as we will see.

In a few cases, these two-storey buildings had quite other uses, as at Hillesden in Buckinghamshire and Roos in Holderness, where they served as rooms from which local lords could follow the mass through openings into the chancel while being largely hidden from the lower orders, though able to keep a wary eye on them too as they milled about the church. But the great majority of these buildings were put up to cope with a wealth of materials almost unimaginable now. They are quite large inside too, as they needed to be. They would have contained several suits of vestments (a suit being all the vestments and their various apparels needed for all three celebrants of mass at the high altar, the sub-deacon, deacon and priest, in the different colours and quality of finishes needed for each season or grade of feast), whole sets of copes to be worn in the quire-stalls (to be exchanged with or worn on top of choir cloaks), surplices to be worn by boy and adolescent singers and other *choristas* (those who worked in quire and sanctuary, carrying incense, candles and books), and the uniforms of water-carriers, thurifers and cross-bearers. In addition, a secure treasury would be needed to contain the other and even more precious gold, jewelled and silver items provided by the people, as laid out in Archbishop Peckham's or Bishop Quivil's early C14 constitutions.

Road widening in towns sometimes involved the demolition of those NE buildings that had been essential to churches with large stores of goods, as at St Mary, Sandwich in Kent. And they have gone very often also in town churches where land use was at a premium, as at Rye in Sussex and Bridgwater in Somerset. Without a knowledge of these ancillary buildings, our understanding of what went on around the altars and in the quire will be very impoverished, but it needs even more imagination to reconstruct the further buildings required by churches where there was a large staff of *choristas* with elaborate choral and ceremonial functions. Inside or built on to these churches, these annexes included song (rehearsal) and teaching rooms and the boys' dormitories.

Outside the church there would have also been collegiate domestic buildings, only a relatively small number of which survive, though statutory colleges were quite well-spread throughout the country, with an average of three such colleges per county, often in rural locations. There were many other para-collegiate establishments, often in town centres, recogniseable by their cruciform central-tower plans. (Some of these are not now obvious as such, having been rebuilt towards the end of the medieval period with western towers instead, as at Long Melford in Suffolk and High Wycombe in Buckinghamshire.)

These college and para-collegiate churches provided a large potential for teaching at all levels. It has been estimated that there was a grammar school for every 6,500 of the medieval population (a figure disputed in detail by some for whom the idea of a well-educated medieval population seems to be undesirable) and not all of these schools were small : some had up to 200 pupils as in the most famous colleges of all, still in unrecogniseable existence, Bishop Wykeham's twin foundations at Winchester and Oxford. Most of these schools were in some way associated with the larger town and country churches and go a long way to explaining how it was that medieval people could build, make music and trade with a level of expertise hard for us to understand, let alone copy.

WORKING IN THE CHANCEL

The reason and purpose of a chancel can be summed up as the performance of the daily round of offices and the daily masses at the various altars. But this is to simplify greatly what actually happened there. As a general minimum, a small rural church with a small staff would sing the two essential offices of Lauds/Matins and Vespers in the quire and a Mass at the main altar. In a well-endowed town church, a large staff of clerics of all ages and grades would sing all eight offices every day. Its staff of priests and deacons sang masses at low, guild or Lady altars as well as celebrating dawn masses at the morrow altars and Jesus altars at the west side of the rood screen. They or other stipendiary priests also sang masses at those altars endowed as chantries. For the mass at the high altar in the sanctuary, the whole clerical community of priests, deacons and musicians of all ages would be brought together every day at mid-morning.

The above is a generalised description of parochial worship ; this now needs to be refined, because it is too easy to assume that this was an imposed rather than an evolved system. So, first we need to look briefly at the history of the Roman church in England and Wales.

Collegiality

Following the Synod of Whitby and other ecclesiastical councils, customs of the Roman church predominated from the later C7 in what was soon to become an anglo-saxon kingdom. The country was evangelised from collegiate centres called minsters. Collegiality (*colligere,* to bind) was then, and for a long time after, the way of life for groups of priests and other clerics who thus bound themselves into a community. From their minsters and through the manorial system they provided the manpower as a patchwork of dioceses and then what were to become parishes grew up. Although some of the minsters and cathedrals were converted to monasteries by invading Normans who themselves planted church buildings at strategic places (chiefly in towns and ports), intended just like castles to be seen as symbols of their conquering power, the idea of collegiality did not go away. Secular (non-monastic) cathedrals remained collegiate and so it appears did many of the newly rebuilt large Norman town and port churches.

The C20, continuing a slide that started in the mid-C16, has been marked by loss of religion and the consequent reduction of clergy numbers. Now hardly any parish has more than one priest and many groups of parishes in rural areas share one or even a part-time one. It is therefore hard for us even to imagine that there was ever the manpower available to staff a collegiate church in the way that is documented as being typical at the start of the C16. Although a modern cathedral is well-staffed by comparison with parishes, staffing levels even in them now pale in comparison with the 200 or so in such places as Salisbury cathedral or the even greater numbers in the households of prelates such as Wolsey or his contemporary archbishops of Canterbury and London, or that of the prince-bishop of Durham. Right down the line, similar levels were normal, so that the training opportunities for musicians and clerks in even relatively small parishes were considerable.

In addition, from near the start of the C13 statutory colleges were also being set up ; an early one at Ulcombe in Kent may have been the result of an encounter at one of the Magna C(h)arta signing assemblies. Training as well as chantry aims were written into their constitutions. Thanks to the punctilious nature of such prelates as Grandisson of Exeter who set out to micro-organise his college foundation at Ottery St Mary in Devon as well as his then relatively-new cathedral foundation at Exeter, we know a great deal about how these places were organised, run and staffed. When links between local colleges and the two university towns were first established in the 1380s by Bishop Wykeham of Winchester with his twin foundations dedicated to Mary, one near his (monastic) cathedral and the other at Oxford, his statutes also described the intended daily life of these colleges in detail.

During the following C15, other prelates and aristocrats followed, founding about 170 statutory colleges of all sizes thoughout the country, again with detailed instructions about how these should be run and how their aims should be achieved. This was at a time when the monasteries had, outside the large towns anyway, mostly lost the lead in recruitment, training and the care of the present and future of aristocratic souls. Many colleges were founded in parish churches, often by adding on magnificent chancels and housing for the extra clergy involved, but sometimes by rebuilding the whole church as a sophisticated combined parish and college building, a classic and neat example being that at Shottesbrooke in rural Berkshire. Meanwhile, also towards the end of the C14, parishes joined in with the effort made by the whole Church to challenge Lollardry and abuses described by Langland in Piers Plowman, not so much by trying to extirpate the heresy (as it was seen) but by raising its own game. Music, ceremonial and ornaments – and staff of all ages from six upwards – poured into churches.

Around half of medieval churches were partially or wholly rebuilt from this time onwards, taking advantage of new techniques but still mindful that these buildings were dedicated to daily sung worship and therefore had to be designed for this work. Their staff were now highly trained and as a result were mobile – upwardly when possible – in a crowded professional market where only the most accomplished rose to the top.

Gradually the collegiate-church idea faded as the numbers of statutory colleges and chantry-college foundations at Oxford and Cambridge increased, supplanting the former system of teaching houses and halls there. We can trace this in the architecture of parish churches too, as we will see. At the Reformation, college churches fared worst of all since their fabrics were designed to favour their founders' college chapels, the east end of most of these churches. Just as Lady chapels in such places as Norwich's cathedral-monastery were allowed to fall down, whole college chancels fell into ruin or were deliberately demolished by the purchasers of former college lands from Edward VI and his advisers. One of the most painful instances of this is the church end of the former royal and aristocratic college of Fotheringhay in Northamptonshire, now a mere stump, the surviving (later) nave representing about a third of the original building. Chancels at, for instance, Attleborough in Norfolk and the huge chancel and chapter house of the college at Howden in east Yorkshire were also victims. Fortunately, the social aspirations of these eradicated communities, dedicated among other things to education and high musical standards, with the finest composers in the land on their staffs, were in a sense already memorialised in a way that may be seen in very many churches up and down the country.

String courses

For the first few years of our research, we naturally noticed the existence of string courses but without giving them a second thought – along with many other things that we now realise are so important to a fuller understanding of the medieval chancel. Then one day on a visit to the former college and parish church at Wingham, situated between Canterbury and Sandwich in Kent and whose master in the 1530s was Edmund, Thomas Cranmer's brother, I noticed something strange while measuring and sketching its college chancel. Its string course at one point terminated in a broken ornament. While I was trying to work out what the ornament was, I further noticed that the course, which visually consisted of just the edge of what turned out to be a quite wide slab of stone, was made of Bethersden 'marble', a dark grey fossilised limestone chiefly known in its native Kent as an ornament in post-Reformation chancel tombs. A quick check showed that the whole of the string course, which ran right round the ample chancel, was made of this material. Soon after this we discovered that Orthodox churches are still designed with a prominent band running round churches as a visible representation of 'the girdle of Christ' that binds together the community of the church.

Not long after, we were visiting the small church at what turned out to be the appropriately-named Norton Subcourse in Norfolk. Here, the string course in the chancel (rebuilt to accommodate the college c1380) stopped dead and without ornament on both south and north sides of the chancel where it would have come up against the now-missing rood screen. The same was true on the outside of the church, where the string course stopped at the west end of the chancel. Now the penny dropped, and from then onwards we have always looked carefully to see how this 'ornamental' course runs. It must be a significant ornament, because it often runs along the tops of quire stall reredoses then up over doorways, dips down under side-window sills and up again over sedilia or piscina or just below the east window sill where retables might have been. Down it goes again where retables' edges may have been. These elastic strings seem to be quite determined to be continuous despite all the various obstacles that other architectural items have placed along their path. A remarkable example of their seemingly innate, almost animal, zeal not to be interrupted is at Sandiacre church

near Derby. Its magnificent early C14 chancel, almost absurdly tall compared with its squat but very wide Norman nave, was it seems built by two teams of masons, one on each side of the chancel. They clearly had their own idea of what profile a string course should have, so where these two different courses meet in a corner of the sanctuary there is an almost risible feat of masonic contortion. But this absurd joint makes the point : that the string has to be an unbroken girdle, come what may.

At the time of writing, we have visited all but a very few of the statutory college churches and chapels. In every one of these, this sign is present with equal continuity except where broken by later tombs on the inside or drain-pipes on the outside. It can also be found in other churches that are not statutory colleges at all, most often in churches such as town-centre cruciform churches where transepts and sometimes naves too have such ornaments. Finding string courses in these has led us to believe that these churches, being so often the linear descendants of minster collegiate churches, also preserve in these stone courses a memory (and therefore presumably the medieval practice) of collegiality.

However, from about the last half of the C15 onwards, this sign seems to disappear in new 'late-perpendicular' buildings, as if the idea had been lost. Perhaps with the extension of collegiality into university education its original meaning of a group of local priests and clerks linked together for mission and education had become diluted. But, as we have said to a number of today's priests-in-charge of churches which have these string courses, there are sermons and lessons in these stones.

THE ACOUSTICS OF CHANCELS

Proportions

In our surveys we have measured the sizes of chancels because first of all their dimensions tell us how many people they were was designed to house and, perhaps more usefully, its proportions of floor area to height tell us what acoustic conditions it was designed to create and foster. My own experience of both singing and working with organs (tuning and sometimes voicing them) in great cathedrals and in the smallest church yard chapels in seven countries in NW Europe for over 60 years tells me that optimal conditions for singing are absolutely essential to make the huge medieval singing work-load of up to several hours a day at all feasible, let alone bearable. A building that fights the singer for any reason – too absorbent (where the singer's output is lost in carpets or wall-hangings, for example) or where the pitch of a sound goes down or, more rarely, goes up as it moves around the building - becomes a battleground where the singer ultimately cannot hope to win a decent performance. It is certain that medieval designers of churches, themselves brought up as musicians, will have placed a suitable acoustic environment for the performance of the daily offices and liturgies at the top of their wants-list. We frequently found when measuring them that C13 and C14 chancels have double-cube proportions, their width and height to their wall-plates being the same and their length being twice this dimension. These *a priori* favour good acoustics, especially in combination with boarded-in wooden or plastered ceilings.

This is a point of view, concerned with the architecture of acoustics, which quite naturally you will not find in architectural histories or indeed much writing about churches. Historians do not usually understand much about the performance of music and musicians are too often poor in their understanding of history and – perhaps surprisingly – of acoustics, too. It has been possible to write whole books about medieval chancels or colleges, or even the whole Reformation period or its chief proponents, without much if any mention of music at all. On the other hand, musicology has too often concerned itself with minutiae of written-down music, forgetting that, for centuries, music was not sung from anything written down but by heart, and according to varying traditions that had inevitably been shaped by buildings with their idiosyncratic acoustic conditions.

The ideal acoustics for singing unaccompanied plain-chant and its improvised elaborations, the daily diet of the medieval musician on which all other later written elaboration was based, would have changed as the music itself gradually evolved. A building suitable for simple monodic plainchant is a resonant one, warming up the tone of the chant and allowing it to form its own sub-melodies by the prolongation of those notes in the chant that are naturally accentuated or which co-incide with any resonant hot-spots in the building. Every group of singers will have found the range of pitches where their building did the most work in supporting and embellishing their work. This range will vary according to the size of the building and the materials used to construct it, no two buildings responding in the same way to similar pitch and tonal outputs. But that does not matter ; plainchant is totally flexible, not only because it is unaccompanied but also because its performance pitch-range can (and should) be adjusted to the building. Only during the C14 when organs became more common in churches other than major monasteries and cathedrals would any firm decisions about pitch have to be made. Even then these decisions would be made to optimise the performance in the building concerned and would not have been made with any reference to a fixed pitch standard. (This would have been impossible anyway before 1711 and John Shore's invention of the tuning fork.)

So one might expect that the eastern parts of churches built for monodic plainsong would be quite resonant ; those churches with vaulted Norman or Early English ceilings or those 'cieled' (sealed) with plaster are ideal. But historically there was an accelerating move towards rebuilding chancels which were often long and relatively narrow into eastern parts which became wider and more complex. Aisles with altars (Lady and guild ones) were added and open arcades were created between them and the quire. As a result, a resonant acoustic changed to one where a singer would have still hoped for a warm response from the building but where there was more clarity. This would be appropriate for the later written-down music, more complex and therefore with singers needing to hear others' musical lines.

Light

As music became more complex, no longer always improvised but with long masses and antiphons (anthems) composed for major feast-days or for services in Lady chapels, being able to read this written music would be vital. Indeed, many rebuilt eastern parts of churches seem to show a response to this requirement. Large lightly-glazed 'decorated' windows found from around 1300 onwards in singing chancels, and then becoming typical from the start of the introduction of what we know as the 'perpendicular' style, may or may not have been introduced because there was new pressure to read written music, but the co-incidence is interesting.

But that these decorated windows are found in chancels first, and that the first perpendicular windows were made for a south-oriented cloister at St Paul's cathedral c1345, one of whose functions was to create spaces for reading and studying, does indicate this possibility. It has also to be mentioned that the point of windows is to be able to see inside a building using the light that comes through them, and this applies to the functional chancel as much as any modern plate-glass office or house. Indeed the still-surviving windows of around 1300 allow in much more light than the C12 windows that for instance light the monastic sanctuary and quire of Canterbury cathedral, where until the early C16 complex music was not read and sung in the monks' quire at all. (The professional choir there sang at the Lady and other altars.) These C12 windows at Canterbury were therefore not replaced in the later medieval period, so C19 restorers, liking their rich colours, placed deeply-coloured windows in chancels everywhere, quite forgetting that they were making reading music there a difficult task. (At Canterbury, choir singers can still read their music thanks only to rows of electric lights beaming down from just below the triforium, though some C12 windows there were removed in the early C17 so preachers and those taking services could see to read their books.)

The acoustic virtues of wood

There are two main reasons why the acoustics of the chancels of many English parish churches are poor for music these days. The first of these is the still-increasing prevalence of carpets on their floors, usually installed without permission during the last 50 years. The second is the tendency of C19 restorers to remove what was left of medieval ceiled chancel roofs mostly made of oak and to replace them with absorbent (and dusty) open-raftered Baltic pine structures. The change of wood is not so important here as what would have come down with the original roofs : that is, all traces of the internal configuration of them. Luckily there are sufficient though very scattered examples of how a late-medieval chancel ceiling was designed or how it looked, and there are some documentary references which reinforce these.

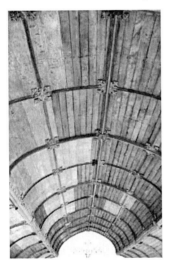

In addition to the acoustic benefits of a double-cube overall shape, a boarded-in roof – in ME parlance, one that is sealed or 'cieled' – whether segmental in shape or, as in many west-country churches, like an upturned cradle or boat, helps to create a favourable acoustic environment. It reflects sound gently back to the singer as well as transmitting sound along the chancel. This would have obvious advantages at the high mass when it is crucial for quire singers and altar celebrants, especially when these latter spoke or sang in a low voice, to hear each other well. In churches with chancel arches that were blocked by tympanum doom paintings, any such transmission would stop there before reaching the nave, as it would if there was an intervening tower space in a cruciform church with two screens, which would have an insulating effect. Presumably though, a west-country church without a chancel arch would also allow some of the sound through there too – if not stopped by hanging paintings or interrupted along the ridge of the ceiling by a celure over the rood.

These ceilinged quires and sanctuaries had extra acoustic help. In the quires, a hollow cove stretched out east-wards from the springing of the uprights of the rood or quire screen, with a solid balustrade placed over it. Together with the back of the doom, these would reflect sound back into the quire and possibly slightly amplify it. In addition, behind each back-row quire stall was also usually a flat board of oak, often painted with the figures of saints, called in ME a 'reredos', this word meaning something placed behind the canon-singer's rear or back. (Its later and present meaning, usurping the ME words table or retable, hardly makes sense.) Over these reredoses rose a tabernacle-like curved canopy with more or less elaborate decoration.

Acoustic jars

In some places, large clay jars similar to Greek *amphorae,* with long necks and fat bellies, were placed horizontally either under the quire stalls or in side walls high above the singers. There are most probably many more of these still waiting to be found under plaster. Their purpose has been much discussed, some tests seeming to show that they did not amplify the voices as much as might be expected. But this is making the supposition that this was the reason for having them. Other acoustic studies that have been done on them might equally suggest that they were there to filter out unwanted acoustic freaks such as unnatural peaks in middle to high frequency reponses from the building. Those buildings where such jars have so far been found are places where there would have been proficient, sophisticated and sensitive musician-singers, those most likely to insist that such anomalies should be rectified. Examples of these include Lyddington in Rutland, next door to one of the bishop of Lincoln's manor-residences, St Clement's in Sandwich, the major church in an east Kent port town, and Leeds in Kent, near a priory and a royal castle.

Carpets

The only carpet known to have been admitted into medieval chancels was a small and costly one, often said to be from 'Turquey' or similar, placed over the '(foot) pace', the step just in front of the high altar. But there were quite a few other fabrics there too, apart from the vestments worn by officiating clergy or the surplices of junior clerics (the *'choristas'*, those who worked in the quire) and the quire singers' thick robes, amuces (fur collars) and hats. The presence of so much clothing probably would have affected the acoustics, though this would be only for the daily high mass, the other offices being confined to the quire where the priests wore choir cloaks or, with the choir singers, quire copes on festival days.

Colour

There was a huge emphasis on colour in every medieval church, almost all traces of which have now been lost. Medieval churchmen had strong ideas of what was and what was not appropriate in a church building, and above all of the 'solemnity' with which it should be furnished, used and maintained in good order. But their word 'solemnity' means 'serious and professional' in modern English, not 'dull' or 'boring'. No statues, no ceilings or roofs and their bosses and corbels and no screens or organs would have seemed complete to the medieval eye without colour. Thanks to studies of the scraps of colour that remain on statues on the façades of various cathedrals from Wells to Amiens and further south, we do know something about how the various medieval colour theories were put into practice. We are also fortunate in England and Wales to have some rood screens that still have their original, or later versions of original, paint still on them. We would have had far more if many screens had not been removed (often without permission) by C19 restorers from churches during the many months it took to 'restore' them and were never put back. (C19 architects and their clients caused the loss of far more screens of all kinds than all three previous centuries of reform.) We would also have far more screens with their original colours if the Camden Society (later the Ecclesiological Society) had not recommended a product supplied by a tradesman of Stowmarket in Suffolk. This was capable of removing all traces of paint from screens or other wooden structures or ornaments, leaving them in their brown oak nakedness, ready to be varnished if architect and incumbent agreed that they might remain as not forming too much of a barrier between the people now in their new pews and the choir in theirs.

The whitened walls, scraped stonework and pickled brown woodwork now contrast with the colour of mostly C19 stained glass in a reversal of the original conception. Medieval walls were vibrant with colour and figures of saints and angels, and bosses and corbels were actually

Lawford in Essex, view from SE, showing plastered Church (left) with one S window to light the rood and a C14 chancel with large windows all round, so that light there is very strongly favoured.

Kelling in Norfolk : N wall of chancel ; note (l to r), remains of foundations of an east wall, the back of the Easter Sepulchre, blocked with uncut flints ; see also p24), a possible wind-trunk hole (high, with red brick infill) and the blocked doorway to a former sacristy.

Music made visible in a flight of angels across the sanctuary ceiling of Gloucester abbey.

Though relegated to the nave and no longer a proud gospel carrier in the sanctuary, this friendly bird at Leverington in Cambridgeshire still keeps an eye open.

Fingringhoe in Essex: statue of a saint and dragon as found under plaster.

Ulcombe in Kent : crucifixion wall painting, north side of Church.

Cawston in Norfolk : east end of the NE chantry ceiling with traces of frescoes on its left wall.

Audignon, Landes, France : the 'English retable' ; note the width of the original mensa now in white in the lower centre. The wood carving of Our Lady is not original to this, but all the paintings are.

Below is a detail of some of these, with their original colours, and traces of gilding on the stonework.

Patrington in Holderness, Lady altar with retable.

Suffolk rood celures or canopies of honour, at Stowlangtoft

and Woolpit, with celure window.

Altar celure, N chancel aisle, Ludlow in Shropshire.

Dooms at Houghton Conquest in Bedfordshire (above) and Stoke by Clare in Suffolk (lower ; possibly Marian period).

visible and readable because of the way in which they were coloured. Celures over altars and the rood were especially ornamented with gold-leaf as well (see colour plates) ; gold stars shone from chancel ceilings, or ceilings were totally-painted with iconographical scenes or angels.

The medieval church was a riot of colour. The little church of St Teilo, removed to St Fagan's Country Park near Cardiff, has been restored with (modern) fresco paintings all over its walls, a rood screen with painted dado and parapets, a large crucifix, and a chancel one cannot enter. Reactions of visitors to it are often quite hostile. Not surprisingly, partly because of shock at the reversing of expectations (coloured walls, light windows) and partly because we can no longer understand the meaning of the fresco figures. In a medieval church such paintings and all that surrounded them were chosen according to a definite programme. The intention was that those who saw them on entering the church or *ecclesia* would be alerted to their own deficiencies and would then be led along a path of salvation and healing towards the quire, the place of heavenly music which was reverently approached under the depiction of Jesus' saving death. Such churches as have been studied and found not to have their surviving iconography seriously disturbed (as it often was during C19 work) tend to show evidence of such schemes, which are paralleled by the didactic arrangement of pilgrimage paths or those to holy sites, shrines and wells.

Carved wooden or stone saints on their corbels near altars or in their niches would all have been painted to be as life-like as possible. (The ME word 'tabernacles' survived to be used by the AV bible translators of the exclamation of those disciples who wished to erect tabernacles for Jesus and the prophets on a high mountain at the Transfiguration.) Their clothes were reproductions of the richest contemporary garments possible, depicting those available under sumptuary (clothing-style) laws only to the highest in the land. Vestments themselves would not have been much behind, as we know from the astonishing embroidery (opus anglicanum) created in workshops in London, Norwich and other major centres and from descriptions of mass vestments and choir copes in inventories and bede-roll accounts. Damasks were only one of the richest of the many imported textiles and dyed silks and gold threads that were used in making these.

Back to the music

The music itself did not lack colour either ; such as escaped destruction in 1548 shows that it was not only ravishingly kaleidescopic to the ear but looked like a rainbow on the page too. Sophisticated and highly-wrought late-medieval music is also immensely varied and colourful in every sense ; it sounds more like organ music improvised in a masterly way and on a large scale. It is wayward, almost romantic, with unexpected touches of harmony and form. It wings its way upwards like the squadron of angel musicians high above the sanctuary of the former abbey at Gloucester.

ORGANS

'The playing of the merry organ, sweet singing in the quire'. Everyone knows this (modernised) carol, but the idea that very many medieval churches actually possessed merry organs of their own seems to surprise those we meet on our research visits. When we say that we are looking for signs of medieval musical infrastructure, most people we come across understand that we might be looking at medieval quire stalls, or they perhaps have a vague notion about acoustics and building shape and can even see, once we mention it, that present vestry buildings were also formerly used to store vestments, treasures and ornaments. But the idea that medieval sanctuaries included an organ and its gallery or 'loft', and that there is evidence that they were there, comes as quite a revelation.

In fact our research in buildings as well as in documents started with the accidental discovery of the supports for a medieval organ gallery and its access in a Suffolk church. This was followed quickly by discovery of similar evidence in three more churches in that county, one of these still housing part of an actual medieval gallery. Another Suffolk church still had unmistakable evidence of where the wind needed to make an organ work was generated.

A pair of organs

ME for 'organ' was 'a pair of organs', a phrase translated from the Latin plural 'pars organorum'. Much ink has been spilt in explaining this phrase, but it cannot be explained satisfactorily without some knowledge of where organs were placed or how large they were. The phrase itself also needs to be unpicked a bit. The word 'pair' in ME, as documents such as CWA and especially inventories show, does not mean something made of two identical things (like a pair of scissors or trousers, neither of which then existed in their modern form) but two things that are complementary and indissociable. A medieval vestry would be the place to find a chalice and its paten, and a censer (thurible) bowl and its chains, both of these being referred to in documents as pairs. Even the triple Godhead of Father, Son and Holy Ghost is referred to as a 'pair' in the carol, 'There is no rose of such virtue,' as having *pari forma*. The word 'pair' does not mean 'two identical bellows' either, as has also been supposed – bellows should anyway never be made indentically for good technico-acoustic reasons – but arises from the fact that every organ is made from two distinct parts that depend on each other's existence to produce music.

Organ lofts

We have found evidence that organ galleries were placed in the sanctuary on otherwise blank north walls above and to the east of the door into the vestries on that side

of the building. These galleries were not deep from north to south ; an organ can be made that takes up no more on the ground than an upright piano – no wider than its keyboards' width and no deeper than a keyboard inside its own casework - plus room for the player on his seat. But their access could be as wide as was available, and above the keyboards the organ casework could broaden out and rise as high as the building allowed, with its pinnacles stretching up into the canted, ceiled

roof above it. Since it is clear that in most places it was one of the singers who played the organ – he had been trained to do this as part of his education as a *chorista* – it was natural that access to the organ gallery was straight from the nearest quire stalls. These stalls, as we have seen, often used the whole space between the rood screen and the western edge of the vestry doorway. The organ player reached the gallery using either steps or a short near-vertical ladder, depending on the space available, or via a doorway through the wall from an adjacent vestry loft.

Bellows lofts

By contrast, bellows take up much more floor space than the foot-print of the organ in its loft in the sanctuary. They can creak a bit when lifted as well as when descending under the pressure of weights placed on them, medieval bellows being more like forge bellows than the ribbed C18 and later ones we are more used to seeing. (These bellows, which create wind are not to be confused with the reservoirs in present-day organs which store wind already created by electric blower turbines or (rarely) by 'pumping' bellows-like feeders under them.) The person or persons operating them would be highly distracting if visible from the quire or sanctuary. Putting them in a separate building with a wind-trunk running through the wall between bellows and organ is a sensible way of dealing with these two problems. We have found evidence of this solution in many places, from major institutions like Winchester college to small rural churches.

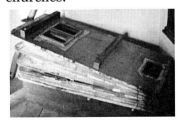 

This separation of the two parts of the organ, its wind-raising and the part that by the agency of the player uses the wind, two different operations both essential to the ultimate result of making musical sounds, seems to be the most likely reason that ME documents continued to use the Latin and English plural 'organs' for one instrument. Two distinct, separated but complementary and indissociable 'parts' make up the necessary 'pair'.

Portatyffs

Tall, fixed organs on lofts were not the only ones found in churches. Many documents refer to a smaller organ which seems to have been moveable if necessary, and is therefore referred to in ME as a 'portatyff'. This emphatically does not mean the tiny arm-held organ associated with (mostly) C19 depictions of St Cecilia, patron of church music despite her martyrdom to the sounds of the Roman amphitheatre organ, but the term included fairly substantial organs – those made in recent years, based on two fortunately-surviving relics of Marian organs found in Suffolk are all organs of this sort. (These reconstructions are indeed always on the move, not just around one church but from one place to another.)

Although we have evidence of these actual late-medieval portatyffs in addition to documents concerning them, including a tuning contract, all the evidence for the larger fixed gallery organs is, with one exception, either documentary or available only from discoverable traces of their siting. Some later-medieval organs, and some much earlier ones, still exist elsewhere in NW Europe, but in England we can get an idea of their scale only from knowing where they were placed – so having some idea of how large they could have been – and how much they cost, and from the music that was likely to have been played on them.

Organ music

There are quite a few references to 'organ books' in later
medieval inventories from the later C15 onwards, but not
a single example seems to have survived the 1548 and
later destruction of Latin music. This is extremely
frustrating, because even one of these would have told us
so much about how the organ was played, perhaps in
contrast (or not) with the singing that was going on in
the same building, or how much of its work had become
in some sense accompanimental by the later medieval
period. We think that at least until the later C15 organs
tended to be played alternately with the singing of
plainsong (simple or embroidered with improvised
descant ? - the latter seems more likely since organs
would tend to be in more sophisticated establishments),
taking a 'verse' (a turn) with the singers in psalms or
canticles. But with the rise of written-down structurally-
complex music, two things (not irreconcileable) are
possible, especially because at this time there are
documentary hints of there being dedicated organ
players whose job is now no longer primarily what it had
been, to sing.

The sort of choir music compiled for Eton college c1490
and for Canterbury cathedral as late as around 1540
often sounds like organ music, with its layering of
sounds, its contrasts between upper voices and lower
ones and their coming together in weightily-structured
passages. For centuries since then, there has always
been an actual or potential cross-over between organ and
choral music, as instanced in the continually-published
transcriptions for organ of choral and solo set-pieces
from Handel's oratorios. One can also well imagine that
the general and highly characteristic tendency for
English organ music to be lyrical rather than massive or
intricate has deep roots. It is difficult indeed to say
sometimes if a piece of late C15 or early C16 music (with
or without words) originated as, or was used specifically
and only as, organ or choral music. 'Choral' music that
consists of many scale passages set against slow-moving
plainsong lines actually looks like organ music and

'organ music' with simple motifs woven into a series of quotations of plainsong lines (with a texture like prototype choral preludes) often resembles a post-Reformation anthem or something written for a consort of viols.

Organ pedals

The mention of slow-moving plainsong lines above brings us to a discussion of pedals. Again, most organ historians – arguing absence of material from absence of evidence – insist that English organs did not have pedals. But a late C14 organ and parts of other organs from the Swedish island of Norrlanda (now in the National Historical Museum in Stockholm, with a restored copy exhibited at Ostheim in Germany) include pedal boards with their own actions and therefore (now missing) pipes. Pedal-playing was referred to in relation to an organ in Florence in 1379, so pedalboards were not exactly unknown in northern and southern Europe. They would not have been unknown in an England which traded with both of these places. Indeed, it is quite possible that an extra keyboard was valuable as what we would now call a 'registration aid' before the system of stops to alter an organ's output became wide-spread or even invented.

Organs and voices

Organs were among the most expensive pieces of equipment of a later-medieval church, along with elaborate rood screens, retables and large hand-written and illuminated antiphoners. Their widespread use in churches of all kinds seems to date from the first of a number of technological inventions made during the C14. Before then organs were basically noise-machines. Written accounts of organs used at Durham cathedral monastery and elsewhere on special days are definitely on the 'merry organ' end of the spectrum of sophistication. These organs were played using pulled or pushed key-sliders which could send wind into up to fifty pipes at the same time. Once however the possibility of modulating the output of organs became possible with the introduction first of finger keyboards and then the possibility of stopping off ranks or sets of pipes (originally by means that are not yet clear), the organ became an instrument which could be used in close proximity with voices ; indeed it would have been 'voiced' (we still use this word) to sound like voices. And since we have some idea of what was expected of singers in terms of vocal output and quality from several sources (including 'mellifluous' and 'dove-like'), we might also have an idea of how these organs sounded.

We can also be sure that they were tuned at whatever pitch was current in any given location, to suit the tessiture of the local singers. They would then be ready to be used in alternation with voices, or – as we know they were – used on high feasts or at special weekly services such as vespers of Our Lady. On special feasts no doubt the player would perform as any modern organist would, as for instance in the Easter Day liturgy at the start of the Gloria in Excelsis, a piece which had not been sung during the several weeks of Lent : that is to let rip with some especially joyous sounds. In town and large churches he would have the extra excitement of the addition of reed (trumpet-like) ranks of pipes at his command. It is not certain if the organ in medieval England was not generally used in Lent ; after all, the important (for the English) feast of the Annunciation on March 25th always fell during Lent, and we have documentary evidence that organ players were paid that day. It is not certain either if organ cases in England always or ever possessed large shutters which would allow them to be closed up during Lent and Advent. If they did have shutters they would be likely to have been painted, and there is no documentary sign whatever that such paintings were taken off and sold once organs started to be 'removed' from sanctuaries for either practical or ideological reasons. This might be because such paintings would have been of forbidden 'images', but no such paintings survive of definitely English provenance and triangular in shape (like wings, rather than square or rectangular), as far as I know.

Organs were the only instruments admitted into churches, or at least into their chancels, to be used for offices and liturgies. Other instruments which are depicted in sculpture, opus anglicanum or glass are indeed those in contemporary use, and they are often drawn with life-like fidelity even if the figures that play them are sometimes either delightful or sordid caricatures, presumably of the actual musicians known to the sculptors and artists concerned. These other instruments would have been used in the *ecclesia* perhaps. They certainly were used around the towns and villages and on their 'pageants', the carts or floats from which sacred and other dramas were presented scene by scene. Or perhaps during dramas played out on the flat roofs of later medieval church buildings ?

The little organ associated in our minds with St Cecilia may represent an actual instrument used in non-church music. It is fairly easily portable, but really needs to be placed onto a table or cart to be fully practical. If one was going to play 'organ music', then it might be more usefully done in the open (or in a nave) with a larger instrument, such as a small portatyff, which would be more likely to make a real musical effect rather than being another sonic version of a fife or recorder-type flute. Such an organ seems to be that portrayed on a cart pulled by a donkey (?) in a carving high on the outside of Alkerton church in Oxfordshire. Indeed, it seems to me that the small St Cecilia 'organ' is actually, where it

appears in medieval iconography, just a small representation of the large pair of organs, miniaturised for emblematic reasons as an attribute of this saint, possessing as it does the two essential parts of a pair of organs : a bellows to raise wind and pipes controlled by a keyboard or button-board to consume wind. Representations of larger organs are not very common for perfectly understandable reasons – chiefly, their size and complexity – though it is interesting that in at least three instances known to me they are each represented from two points of view in separate carvings or drawings, the better to give some idea of their size perhaps, and certainly of their complexity.

Large English organs

By the end of the medieval period, English organs were large as well as complex. We know this from two valuable contracts for large organs in parish churches in the City of London and in Coventry, and from a Hollar engraving of a late-medieval organ at St Paul's cathedral as well as from the lucky survival of a dated organ apparently made for Westminster abbey when it was turned into a cathedral in 1540. This organ was moved to St Brieuc cathedral in northern Brittany towards the end of the C16 and although its case now contains another organ, some of its original pipework is in another organ near Tréguier. All of these instruments needed to have been physically large to contain the costly

and therefore complex organs whose technical contents are partially described in the contracts.

The St Paul's organ was up to 25 feet or possibly more in height as drawn, standing on one of the quire 'gradus' there. The Westminster/St Brieuc organ is somewhat taller, and is as wide as it is tall, with complex highly-carved casework and an arrangement of front pipes that anticipates all the styles of the next two centuries. If its casework profile is at all typical of what was being made in England then, truly England was far ahead of others, though its carved decoration is Spanish plateresque or Italian renaissance in style. Laying out a lot of money in design and construction of its organs was one of the ways in which larger cities and towns approached the task of doing their best for their churches' worship. At Southwold, a rich trading port on the Suffolk coast, a large opening in the north wall between quire and sanctuary was made for a late-medieval organ and loft in the same style as extensions to the eastern parts of the sanctuary were built in the late C15. So this organ presumably dates from this time, as would have the organs in other Suffolk port churches at Covehithe and Walberswick, traces of whose organ galleries and their access also remain. At Southwold there is (as in Winchester college's chapel) ample room behind the opening for the several organ bellows which would have been needed for a sizeable instrument played at full tilt.

Did your church have a medieval organ ?

If your church once included (or still has) a NE building, it would have be tall enough to have a 'loft' floor in it above the vestry or sacristy into which at least two bellows and their operator could be fitted in. The work of their operator was not to pump them in the way familiar from smaller organs made from the mid-C18 onwards, to work a pivoted handle that raises feeder-bellows alternately. Manipulating earlier styles of wedge-bellows requires somewhat more subtlety. The operation starts by lifting one of the bellows to open it, usually by means of a lever which is pushed down, the other end rising and attached to the top of the bellows' opening end. CWA often mention the purchase of ropes for an organ, so it seems likely that in many cases bellows were lifted by pulling down a pole or rope attached to the lever suspended from a roof beam whose other end was attached by a pole or rope to the bellows. Some sort of lever or gearing system is necessary because every time the bellows is raised, not only the weight of the wooden top of the bellows has to be lifted but also the lead weights that lie on the bellows to pressurise the wind, and the larger the bellows the more weights it has to carry to give the same pressure of wind. So his work is made easier by allowing the pull by the operator to go over a longer distance, often twice that of the rise of the opening bellows.

Lifting the first bellows causes air to be drawn into it by suction through valves in its underside. When the bellows is at its highest, the operator needs to let go carefully of the lever so as not to jog the wind. This first bellows then starts to go down as wind is taken out of it by the organ player or by natural leakage. When it has got about two-thirds of the way down, the operator lifts the second bellows, and again when it is fully open gently lets it go to ensure a smooth flow of wind. As the air in the first bellows is exhausted, the descent of the second bellows covers the time that it takes to bring up the first again. This alternation is repeated, with the operator never letting both bellows become empty so causing the organ to stop sounding.

The speed at which each bellows drops depends on the amount taken out by the organist ; if he plays many ranks of pipes at once or uses full chords the operator has to work more quickly. As in fact the pressure of wind forced out through the bellows increases slightly as the bellows descends, the operator could have a subtle (or not so subtle) influence on the phrasing of the sound of the organ, forcing the pipes to get very slightly louder as the bellows get near the end of their travel downwards. But the organ maker should have taken care to make sure that the overall capacity of the bellows is sufficient for all demands. A larger organ will inevitably have more than the minimum two bellows and if there are four or more bellows another operator would be needed. As well as the creaking and visual distractions of the whole business of blowing an organ this way noted before, when there are more than two bellows the operator has to move around between them. This can create more noise, this time of footsteps on a wooden floor, giving another reason for having the bellows in a separate place, acoustically insulated from the sanctuary and organ.

Pressurised wind from the two or more bellows is pushed into a collecting wind-trunk placed along their ends and then has to go through to the organ on the other side of the wall. This means that the wall is pierced with a square hole with a wind-trunk (a square or slightly rectangular wooden tube, originally a tree-trunk, hence its name) going through it. The height of this trunk and the bellows is arranged so that the wind goes as directly as possible into the soundboard, the wind-distribution part of the organ that lies inside the organ case, not far above the head of the player, and on which all but the largest and front pipes of the organ sit. The trunk would need to come through the wall at about 13 feet (4m) from the floor level of the sanctuary, so any anomalies in the wall at around this height, if this wall is unplastered on the outside or de-plastered on the inside, might show where the wind-trunk came through. There is a soundboard for each keyboard, so larger organs might need to be deeper or wider or much taller to accommodate more than one of these. It seems likely that most organs made for average-sized parish church sanctuaries would have just the one keyboard, with possibly a pedalboard (keys played by the toes) connected to it.

About half of the published CWAs that cover the years up to 1600 make definite mention of organs, but mostly they do so obliquely. They will itemise expenditure on, for instance, 'a cord for the orgaynes' – in other words, the rope connections mentioned above – which will wear out naturally. About every 25 years, so does the sheep or calf leather usually used on these bellows after being continually pulled tight and then crushed with rise and fall of the bellows ; then the cost of repairs to these, involving glue and nails, is also found in CWA.

Size of bellows lofts

Each bellows would have been a minimum of about 5 feet long by around 2 feet 6 inches wide, so a smallest area taken up by just the bellows of a smaller organ if set on their own frame, with the operator standing on the floor below, would be around 6 feet square with around 5 feet in height for the levers. This could be squeezed into the head of the triangle formed by the top of a cat-slide roof that reached up a total of around 15 feet ; in fact, most of these roofs are higher than this at this point, as shown by their surviving corbels. With their operator on the same level as the bellows, the most common method, the minimum floor-space needed would rise to something like 9 feet square, and sufficient headroom for the operator and the levers would be around 10 feet. A cat-slide roof that reached up about 18 to 20 feet would therefore have accommodated bellows and operator on an upper floor or loft ; it would also need stairway or ladder access.

If your church shows signs of any of this – an attached building of the 'right' height and potentially the 'right' overall floor area set behind about 15 or more feet along a blank north wall in the sanctuary, and your CWA mentions 'cords' for an organ - it is likely that it

possessed a fixed organ on a gallery. If these conditions are not fulfilled, then either the organ was a portatyff (whose smaller pair of bellows, lifted by hand without cords, could be moved when the organ was moved around), or was fixed elsewhere in the church, perhaps on a screen-loft near the quire stalls

Size of organ lofts

Most churches are at least 18 or 20 feet tall from the floor level of the sanctuary to the wall-plate that supports the rafters, the angle of the roof ceiling allowing more height at the front of the top of an organ case. If the floor of an organ gallery there was set at about 8 or 9 feet up, most churches would be able to accommodate an organ whose case was between 12 and 15 feet high overall, including cresting decorations and/or pinnacles. But the potential height of an organ placed in a screen-loft, or on one end of a rood-loft (see below) would depend entirely on the heights of arches or ceilings where it was placed.

In Shottesbrooke college's church a north chancel window was blocked when a now-missing NE building was built there, so there is a good chance that there was a later-medieval organ on a gallery in the sanctuary, its wind-trunk going through the otherwise blocked window. Those churches that have now-blocked windows originally installed before the mid-C14 on the north of the sanctuary area and have signs of, or surviving, NE buildings behind these, are therefore likely to have had organs in lofts there and in the sanctuary as well.

Only radar reading of the wall, if it is still plastered, might reveal anomalies in the wall which would be holes for the gallery supports and balustrade or might find the wind-trunk hole, if this is not now hidden behind a post-1570s memorial wall-tablet. By the 1570s most organs had been 'removed' from the sanctuary or chancel and transferred to another part of the church building – if it was kept at all, since the idea that organs were 'popish' was already beginning to gain ground by then. The CWA or other archives will tell you what happened, because the labour cost of dismantling and breaking up an organ is a matter of something around 12 pence (a shilling) whereas the cost of taking it down, refashioning and putting it back up in the nave or perched on the rood screen would have been around five times as much. Nonetheless, and despite the last-ditch (as it turned out) attempts of Laud and Charles I to re-beautify English churches, C17 puritans had convinced themselves that the whole idea of church music was popish. So, in 1644 organs were finally banned by the puritan parliament, along with – astonishingly – fonts as well as any left-over holy water stoups. Although some organs stayed in place for two or three more years in the far south-west, where the government's rule penetrated last, for around the

next fifteen years there was no music worth the name in
English churches.

It took two full centuries for organs to be put back in any
number into churches ; by the start of the C19, only
around 750 churches out of about 12,000 had re-
installed organs. The chain of memory had been thus
comprehensively broken, hence the un-researched
received idea that there were few organs in medieval
churches. But since we know that English music was
prized everywhere for its melodious complexity and the
choirs famed for their high level of competence, it would
be hard to imagine that the *summum* of equally complex
and melodious instruments would not be found
everywhere one could be afforded. The rich trading
nation that was inherited by Henry VIII in 1509, and was
maintained as such until the repeated disasters of the
end of his reign thirty years later, certainly wanted to
have almost everything that could be placed in churches,
and this included organs, made (like stained glass) in
workshops in major and minor towns all over the
country.

My own estimate, based on the totality of our recent
research, is that there were organs of some kind in at
least half of all churches and chapels in the kingdom.
City churches very often possessed two or even three
organs (it is sometimes hard to see where these were
shoe-horned into what were already well-stocked
buildings) and really rich monasteries, churches and

cathedrals had
even more –
as did the
Lincolnshire
port church of
Boston, which
is known to
have had four
or even
possibly five
organs in the
early years of

the C16. There is even documentation for a small Suffolk church still having two organs in the early C17, but where these were placed in a chancel as fully packed with family monuments as this was by then, is very difficult to say. Even more incomprehensibly, these two organs were documented at a time, in the 1620s, when the use of only one organ had to be justified and defended, let alone two.

B is for Barriers

ESSENTIAL to the harmonious functioning of a medieval church building, the various screens which ran across the inside of the building in every church exhibited the plurality of solutions that parishes found to make this barrier a source of visually-compelling instruction in the salvation of the crucifixion of Jesus and the examples of the saints of the church.

Basics of a rood screen

A rood-screen is a complex piece of work, but then it had a number of jobs to do. It was a light but effective, locked separation between east and west parts of the church building, supplanting with ever more elegant designs and fantastic execution previous barriers between *ecclesia* and altars. Earlier barriers had included a complete masonry wall with a doorway and two windows in it, as still at Eastwell in Leicestershire, but they eventually developed into large independent structures made in oak which stretched right across the church and supported (literally) a number of artefacts and even occasionally activities. Most fully-developed screen systems consisted of

(a) the screen itself, its lower part (the dado) comprising panels, often painted with local and international saints and other ecclesiastical figures chosen according to a predetermined iconographical scheme, with above this a series of openings resembling window tracery, capped by a lintel beam.

(b) a platform, usually 5 feet or more wide from west to east with panelled parapets about 3 feet high running along its east and west edges.

(c) above the platform, either on a separate beam or socketed into the eastern parapet, rose the at-least life-size crucifix ('rood' is anglo-saxon for the cross itself, as in the very early poem, 'The Dream of the Rood') and statues of Mary and John. These might have been accompanied by angels and, if the sole-surviving example at Cullompton in Devon was not unique, by gruesome depictions in carved and painted realism of the hill of Golgotha, the place of skulls (execution). Cullompton's Golgotha must have been the (lower?) rood beam in fact, since mortises for statues and the crucifix are in its upper surface, and so it is quite possible that other rood beams were themselves similarly carved. The crucifix must in many cases have been steadied by being held by hooked rods in forged-iron eyes set in the roof or chancel arch above the platform. Sometimes these eyes are still visible, the difficulty of removing being more than they were worth as scrap.

In most churches, any surviving parts of the rood screens are fragmentary and it takes quite an effort of imagination to visualise the complete ensemble, no medieval example of which survived decades of ruthless campaigns against them. More often, only the screen tracery survives, with a horizontal lintel beam stretching at about pillar-capital level either across the chancel entrance arch or across the chancel aisles, or even all of these. On rare occasions the ensemble rises higher with one or two hollow-curved superstructures both sides of the lintel, to the east and to the west. Inside these coves is a very massive structure that holds a series of joists running north to south and, above these, west to east. In a very few surviving instances the curved-cove's structure is simplified. Ornamented joists jettied out westwards and eastwards in the manner of the supports for first-floor lofts in houses. These support the platform, whose floor planks run north to south.

For the low-church C19 incumbent, screens, and especially their painted panels of often non-biblical saints, were relics of a past better forgotten - an attitude still to be found among evangelical congregations, or their leaders. For high-church Tractarians, any obstruction of a good view of their newly-raised neo-counter-reformation altar was to be deplored. As a result, during the C19 England lost around half of its then stock of a highly-characteristic art form, the pride and joy of those who paid dearly for it. It must be remembered though that rood screens were also part of the furnishings of every church under Roman influence throughout NW Europe, and the losses outside England were so severe as to be practically total. It's hard to convince historians in France for instance that their medieval churches also had rood screens. The scrubbed-clean churches of Scandinavia, Germany and Switzerland have also lost all traces of such things – and much more besides.

Present signs

If there's no rood screen now, it is possible that the chancel step is not in its original place. You can check if it is or not by looking at the north and south pillars of the arch. First, look at the bottom of these pillars. Since many rood lofts were either installed within an earlier structure, you may find that the bases of the pillars have been cut back to take a low foundation beam. This crossed between the chancel arch pillars and the whole vertical structure which supported the screen and platform assembly was tenoned into mortises in it. If on close inspection these pillars show signs of in-filling, leaving marks anything up to around 6 inches (150 mm) square, at about 3' (about a metre) up from the floor and in vertical line with the cutting-back of the pillar bases, and both of these are in line with the middle of the present step, then the step is likely to be where it or its medieval predecessors used to be.

If there are no marks at all on the chancel arch pillars, it is likely that the chancel arch has been rebuilt either partly or completely. This is because a late-medieval rood screen might have disguised the lowness or antiquity of a former chancel arch. Removal of the rood assembly would have revealed an 'anomaly', and any C19 architect would have felt it his bounden duty to improve this away. It is likely that the rood loft stairs would then have been removed so that their hollow space could be filled in to provide extra strength to sustain the thrust of a higher and wider C19 arch. This is bad news for the archaeol-ogist, because much of the stonework around the junction of nave and chancel will also have been disturbed or even completely replaced, both inside and outside the church building.

A coved support for the platform would have been much more complex and expensive to make, but in a parish with the resources to have this done, the attraction is clear : it more nearly resembles the style and structures used in chantry chapel surrounds and tombs in the greater churches and cathedrals (and presumably once in monasteries also) and lends itself to more adornment with carving and colour.

In very rare examples, parapets to the platform with their balustrades survive. The western front of the parapet included tabernacle-niches with saints on its western side. Its balustrade was bored with holes for sockets for candle holders and basins for vegetable oils with floating wicks ; these are among the 'lights' for whose sponsors the priest requested prayers in his bede-roll invocations. Apart from a handful of examples on the Welsh-Hereford border, there are no original rood lofts and parapets go right across the chancel arch, all examples in England being confined to side chapels. Relics of such structures are therefore precious and rare, having survived against the odds – mostly because they fronted private chapels whose patrons, having paid for them, presumably had not taken kindly to being told to remove the 'images' in the first place by Henry and Edward and then were sufficiently strong to resist Elizabethan bishops' illegal demands to remove the loft and its parapets as well.

Rood-loft stairs

Now the most-frequently found signs of rood lofts in England, stairs were needed to access lofts to maintain the lights on them. Someone, presumably the sexton or possibly one of the junior clerks, had to douse them at night at the ringing of the couvre-feu (cover the fire or curfew) bell. Only the wax candle at the foot of the crucifix was kept burning, but this could be used to light the other lights in the morning when the basins were also topped up with oil.

Stairs are to be found in all sorts of places : near the chancel arch or at the north or south ends of the screen in the thickness of walls or in turrets built onto them, all depending on what local conditions allowed. In some extreme cases, access was even from the outside of the church, and this is symptomatic of the problems encountered by church wardens and their masons needing to install these stairs into an existing structure. In a newly-built late-medieval church such stairs are clearly designed-in from the start and it is quite easy to spot these, so noting the difference between 'inserted' and 'designed in' stairs will help to date them and the rood-loft assemblies by reference to their surrounding masonry and other features such as windows.

The steps of 'inserted' stairways are almost always narrow at around 18 inches on average, but that average means that some steps are as narrow as 15 inches and some as wide as 21 inches. They are also often steep with steps up to 10 or even 12 inches in height, this being done to minimise the space they take up, since the higher each step, the fewer turns there will be in the spiral stairs. Usually the steps start near ground level, but where it was not possible to turn as much as about three-quarters of a circle they had to start higher, so some might start as high as 30 inches from the surrounding ground level. In which case a short pair of steps would have been needed. Similar constraints also made it necessary for some stairs to the upper rooms ('lofts' too in ME) above porches in the *ecclesia*, and where there are high-starting stairs to these, they might help to indicate when a porch might have been added to an existing fabric or rebuilt with a new loft.

Rood stairway windows and doorways

A majority of rood-loft stairways are not lighted by windows of any kind ; they are too short to need this, but longer ones are provided with openings. Usually these give on to the outside of the church, as would be normal in a stair-turret built into or attached to an outside wall. When the stairs are built within the church though, their windows seem to be arranged so that they not only help light the steps but also allow anyone in the stairway to keep an eye on other parts of the church such as entrance doors, or the high or other altars. As with squints, to find out what these openings might be there for, one needs to go up and see what you can see from them as well as looking at them from outside the stairway.

Lower stairway doorways themselves are often themselves quite low at between 5' and 5'6" and narrow at 21" or less ; usually the size of the upper doorways matches that of the lower ones, except where they are able to be a little taller. Low lower doorways and higher upper ones suggest that one of the designed features, where space was at a premium and choices had to made, was to allow a rapid ascent. Where there are burning wicks and candles fixed to a wooden structure, the reason for this is obvious. That this was considered when designing these stairs can often be confirmed by the ways any original lower doors are hinged in respect of the start of the stairs, or the position of such hinges at the upper level. Lower doors were also locked for equally obvious safety reasons and it seems that normally a rapid ascent was never impeded by locking the upper doors. Needless to say that if original doors or signs of them (hinges or signs of these, and lock- or bolt-holes) can still be found, they need to be interpreted thoughtfully and carefully preserved.

Where exactly loft-stairs start and finish also gives us vital clues as to the arrangement of the east end of the peoples' church, where so often everything else that used to be there is now missing. The sill of the upper doorway – if it has not been blocked and covered with later monuments – indicates, as mentioned before, the likely level of the floor of the rood platform-loft, though in some cases this is not quite the case. We have visited lofts where there was an additional step up onto the platform, which might indicate that the whole assembly was renewed at a later date.

Lower access doors - west or east ?

The most important thing about the placing of the lower doorway is whether it is west of where the screen is (or was) or to its east. If the latter, which it is in only a small minority of cases, this seems to show that those responsible for the lights were more likely to be those who worked in the quire and sanctuary – one of the clerks, perhaps, as mentioned above. If these eastern stairs are also wider than what appears to be normal (that is, 21 inches or more) and less steep (less than 9 inches) as well, and with wide doorways to match, then this is a precious indication that these steps may have been used for other reasons than just looking after the lights on the western balustrade. Previous comment-ators have come up with all sorts of reasons as to why access to lofts, apart from maintenance of lights, might be needed. Few of these are convincing in view of the difficulty clerks and priests would have in getting up the huge majority of them in quire robes and the even greater problems of doing so in sanctuary vestments – and the fact that such access would be the wrong side of a locked screen, too.

However, the sometimes wider stairs from the east do deserve special attention, and perhaps allow us to give some credence to some of the proposals made over the past 110 years about the use of some rood-lofts. Eastern access points are found predominantly in the west country where most churches do not have chancel arches and where the three aisles usually run through the length of the building without interruption, the eastern ends of north and south aisles forming the spaces for chancel side Lady and guild altars. Consequently, in these lofts there is usually more unimpeded height to both to east and to west in all three aisles. The central part of the loft is taken up with the golgotha, crucifix and other statues as well as the normal access to lights along the western balustrades, the walls between the aisles being pierced if necessary to allow for this, or the western edge of the platform being set far enough west to allow access round the nave and chancel pillars and arcades with enough headroom. On a large loft, it might have been possible that (for instance) the passion story in the gospel for Palm Sunday was sung from the centre of the loft. It is even possible that a very small organ was placed to the side of the centre of a very large loft. But lofts in the side aisles would be open and their floors would be unencumbered, and there is often good head-height here too, so it is not difficult to imagine that organs might have been placed here, especially those given by and dedicated to the use of the guilds whose special altars may have been in these aisles.

My main reason for suggesting this is that organs tended to persist in the west country during the later- or post-Reformation periods longer than elsewhere. This may have come about because such organs, well placed to be heard and seen in the nave as well (as no doubt such organs would be intended to have been, right from the start) could immediately and without alteration have been pressed into their new rôle of accompanying the congregational singing of Englished metrical psalms, the hymns of that and later periods.

Screens in quires

Pierced screens, usually with similiar decoration to the lower parts of rood-screens, were set behind quire stalls if there were arches behind the stalls giving on to chancel aisles with their own side altars. (Reredos backs to stalls are always fixed to a solid wall.) There are doorways, giving access to these side altars, at the east end of these quire screens. Such 'parclose' screens are probably overall more common than rood screens, but although many are missing, traces of them can be found on the pillars of the arches between quire and aisles and cutouts in their bases. The east end of Lincoln cathedral for instance, was a maze of parclose screens, none of which are there now.

Pulpitum and quasi-pulpitum lofts

Although rood-loft staircases are very common still, despite C19 rebuildings, there are many places where a church rather surprisingly does not have one, and where destructive rebuilding has not taken place either. Such churches are usually large late-medieval churches, those one would expect to have the most elaborate and expensive rood-loft assemblies. One such place is Salle, which although one of the best-known large churches in rural Norfolk has many things in and around it that have not yet been convincingly explained. Here are signs that the rood assembly was much larger than just a coved rood-loft (signs of a short cove can be seen to the SE side of the chancel arch at the height where the screen's lintel would have been) but there is not and apparently never has been a stone stairway.

Salle church was not subject to C19 restoration but was quite carefully tidied up in the early C20. West of the chancel arch, are large spaces for side altars to both north and south, rather like transepts (though the church was clearly collegiate, it does not appear ever to have had a central tower) and these altars should be considered as part of the clerical church just as in a normal towered-cruciform building. Such altars would have been screened from the people's part of the church, so that the peoples' rood and statues etc would naturally have been placed one bay to the west of the chancel arch and the surviving remains of the screen : its dado and some uprights.

The joinery of this screen at Salle also suggests that it extended westwards, so it seems fair to posit a large competely-independent structure that included a tall screen at the chancel arch (with its cove to the large quire, as mentioned), screens to north and south (towards the quasi-transepts) and to the west, these also going right across the aisles. A stairway (or two) to the loft could easily be contrived to one or both sides of the central enclosed space thus created under a large loft. There would be all the space needed on such a platform for the usual rood, statues etc., and an organ, which we know existed in this church because of an organ book that was itemised in a C15 inventory. (There is no sign of there ever having been a NE building and there is no space for an organ on a wall in the chancel, its fenestration being continuous and complete.)

Such a structure is rather like that described in the contract for a large and expensive structure at Stratton in Cornwall which included side screens in the quire and incidentally a loft for the organ on one of these. But it resembles even more a wooden version of the stone pulpitums still found in some cathedrals, both monastic and secular, such as at Canterbury and York, or the surviving wooden pulpitums at Hexham and Carlisle, and the 1530s screen at King's college, Cambridge. The lofts in these pulpitums were not intended to support a crucifix and Mary and John, but are were built for organs and for liturgical purposes, a 'pulpit' being a singing-desk incorporated into an eastern parapet. They are always accessed by internal stairways. I therefore suggest that similar structures, although now entirely missing, are the only way of explaining how rood-lofts were accessed in the total absence of rood-loft stairs even where these might be expected to have survived.

There are also churches without chancel arches where the easternmost arches are wider and taller than the other arches of otherwise regular arcades. Here, even if there are still stone loft-stairs, it is possible that there would have been an independent pulpitum-like structure whose double screens, going right across the church through the western of these larger arches, enclosed altars in the aisles. They seem to show that what is sometimes now their nave was once part of the clerical area of the church building ; an example is at Broad Clyst near Exeter. Town churches with tall arcades that run continuously from west to east, such as All Hallows Barking by the Tower in the City of London – a church with a very expensive and large early–C16 organ which had to be accommodated somewhere - are also likely to have this sort of quasi-pulpitum arrangement. These variations of the 'standard' loft arrangements once again emphasise that each church designed its own solution to accommodate its requirements as they arose.

Another example of the need for a multi-disciplinary approach to aid understanding of these now-missing structures, is to be found in the parish church of the episcopal stannary town of Ashburton in Devon. Unlike most of the church buildings in that part of England, this has a central chancel arch and chancel aisle arches as well. Here a loft seems to have stretched across the whole space between the chancel arch and the first pillars of the nave, with presumably (in absence of any other stairway) internal stairs as in a pulpitum. CWA there record that when the organ was moved from an unspecified position to another, its removal meant employing a halyer (a roof tiler) to remove tiles to remove hooks or similar steadfasts that held the organ steady, implying that it was high up on some sort of loft, perhaps this one, then being demolished by order. Naturally, in these circumstances CWA tend to be laconic and we have to fill in the gaps as best we can.

Screens in tower spaces

Another possible variation on a large pulpitum-like structure might be the lofts that seem to have been built into the tower areas of cruciform college churches and para-collegiate town churches. A central tower was a useful object, especially in the dual-purpose buildings that most college chancels were fitted onto, having been often added to parish churches, as we have seen. One tower to keep all the bells that both users of the building might need was *a priori* sensible, and disputes such as those between the citizens of Wymondham and the monks into whose monastery their church had been built, leading to the former building a whole new tower, are not found in college histories.

The tower space at floor level is also a useful buffer zone, acoustically and liturgically. Where the staircase up the towers is positioned needs to be noticed ; if (as at, for example, Stratford on Avon in Warwickshire) it is within or near one of the tower's western pillars, then it can serve as the stairs to the parish rood loft as well as access

to the bells, and this seems to be the usual solution in a dual-purpose building. However, para-collegiate staff appear to have needed pulpitums as well, in many cases as places to put organs (which would face eastwards into the quire) where they could not find sufficient wall-space for an organ in a fully-fenestrated quire and sanctuary. They would also have been designed to support a well-developed musical liturgy in which at times part of the staff would have moved to such a loft for didactic purposes such as the dramatised Palm Sunday gospel or for special musical effects.

Lofts in central towers do (or did) occasionally have access stairs leading directly from the quire too, as did the rood screen in Wingfield college church in Suffolk, which has a now-blocked access from a N chancel chapel. A number of tower lofts, or rebuilt versions of them, were still in use to support organs placed on galleries at the east end of the nave during the C18, until they fell victim, perhaps along with valuable archaeological evidence of their former state, in the mid-C19, to the wholesale removal of galleries in churches. Some were photographed, and it would be useful to compare these photographs with the evidence in stonework in these places. All these various elements – position of stairways, absence of stairways, position of lofts, access to the peoples' rood screens and tower bells – have to be taken into account in any particular situation for some sense to be made of what is there and what is missing.

Screens in the peoples' church

Careful search among C19 pews might reveal cut-aways in the bases of pillars that show where 'parclose' screens for altars in the peoples' church had been retro-fitted. As CWA often indicate more altars than could have been possibly incorporated into other parts of the building, careful lining up of what is written with such evidence in the fabric can yield dividends. Some East Anglian churches use the tops of parclose screens as access ways to the platform of the rood screen, though at Dennington the masons had some fun with us, allowing access to the rood from the south but not from the north, although it looks as if there are two ways of getting to the rood loft.

Destroying your own work

Pulling down such large and expensive structures as rood lofts and their statuary by order just because their parapets included niches with images must have been a heart-wrenching experience for church wardens, who themselves might well have witnessed their building or knew all about it from their parents. It is not surprising that in those cases for which we still have continuous accounts for the first decades of the reign of Elizabeth I that it took many years – sometimes a whole generation – of persuasion and threats to force wardens to pay for the removal and disposal of their cherished lofts and pulpitums. They and their screens might now have gone out of sight but they are still part of the memory-history of every church, and usually something remains of them, even the slightest of these signs being informative.

Rood celures and additional clerestory and other windows

Honour was paid to the crucifix and its message of salvation in the same way as altars (and monarchs), by having richly-decorated canopies over them. The survival of such celures is limited, for all sorts of reasons, but it is sometimes possible to see where they had been. Having built such expensive structures they needed to be seen to the best advantage. Even if the nave roof had already been renewed with clerestory windows, there are places where extra windows were installed to increase the lighting, especially onto the crucifix itself. I have the impression, from actual experience in midlands churches, that these windows were even sometimes designed to throw light on the crucifix – or rather on where it once was - especially in the early afternoon (roughly between noon and three in the afternoon in modern timing), at the significant Passion-tide season of the Spring equinox when the sun is at a particular angle in the sky. It would be interesting to know if that has been anyone else's experience in other places.

Elsewhere, extra windows seem to have been punched through the walls to light the loft itself, presumably to make it easier for the person tending to the lights early and late to see as well as possible without the need to carry potentially-dangerous lanterns up into the loft. There was always the rood-foot wax light to relight the other lights from, as we have seen. In late-medieval churches, specially-designed clerestory fenestration, with extra-wide or doubled windows, are clearly there to increase the lighting of the rood and the doom behind it.

Dooms

Very often associated with rood-lofts, a representation of the last judgement was almost ubiquitous in churches. In many churches, this was painted on boards fixed inside the chancel arch (leaving marks on the stonework within the arch), just behind the crucifix. In taller buildings, the doom was painted on the wall above the chancel arch. Even here the crucifix sometimes predominated ; its outline-shadow can sometimes still be seen within the doom painting, as at Cawston and Attleborough in Norfolk. Otherwise, a large area was given over wholly to a complex depiction of the coming pains and griefs or future eternal joys, as at St Thomas, Salisbury or Holy Trinity, Coventry. But there are other places where it is hard to see how and where this dreadful day was depicted. In a west-country church without a chancel arch there is nothing to attach the painting to. Perhaps it was done on cloth and hung up, but I have not seen either documentary or physical evidence for this. A large pupitum-loft would make it difficult to see any such painting unless the chancel arch was unusually tall and had boards within it or the doom was set very high on the east wall of a very tall nave. A number of churches also have windows in the wall above the chancel arch whose purpose was clearly to light the celure over the rood, so a choice had clearly been made not to paint the doom there.

Reconstructing the whole apparatus of salvation (as
those who had it all made would have viewed it) requires
informed and imaginative thought - and measurement.
Careful, considered examination of what is there, finding
what traces are left and remembering that there is much
that is no longer there, are unavoidable tasks for the
historians and guardians of our medieval churches.

C is for the Church

CONTROL BY THE PEOPLE over their part of the building,
the church or *ecclesia*, goes back a long way ; church
wardens are known to have been in post since at least the
C12 century. It is a moot point whether the Church of
England has ever actually legally taken control of this
part of the church building, not maintained by medieval
church authorities - an aspect not considered by the
Sustainability Review panel. Perhaps some reader of this
book may like to clarify this matter, quoting any
appropriate early Acts of Parliament still in force.

Building and maintaining

There are long historical reasons for the peoples' interest
in this end of the church building, one possibly
important factor being that many towers were first built
as beffroi, places of refuge for the whole community in
times of trouble, before church buildings were attached
to them. But their church too was always a community
effort, in its building, maintenance and embellishment,
always in the context of the ultimate purposes for which
the building was created. 'The parish', wrote the C19
Bishop Hobhouse, 'was the community of the township
organised for Church purposes, and subject to Church
discipline, with a constitution which recognised the
rights of the whole body as an aggregate, and the right of
every adult member, whether man or woman, to a voice
in self-government, but at the same time kept the self-

governing community under a system of inspection and restraint by a central authority outside the parish boundaries.'

To say that people were solely in control of their own part is perhaps as wrong as saying that they paid nothing for the eastern part (they paid for the books and ornaments there, for example) but as far as the fabric of each part is concerned this is pretty well correct. Archbishop Peckham had ordained clearly that the parishioners were liable for supplying and repairing (and renewing), among other things : '... the bells with their cords ; a font with its lock and key ; the images in the *ecclesia* ; the enclosure wall of the cemetery ; all repairs of the nave of the church, interior and exterior ; repairs also in regard to the images of the crucifix and of the saints and to the glazed windows...'

Parishioners responded where they could to these requirements, funding or co-funding enormous additions to their part of the building : new aisles, new clerestories with their roofs and ornate ceilings, new porches, towers and spires. In some cases they also funded new lateral altars (transepts in modern English) and all that was needed to furnish them, including their division-screens. Parishioners also paid for the entire rood-loft assembly, whose cost could run into seven figures in equivalent present-day purchasing power.

A large new west tower would cost even more – almost as much as the rest of the *ecclesia* – and take many years to build. It would not have been started until enough funds were in hand to build it up to the height of the archway into the central alley so it could be roofed over temporarily while the money for the upper storeys and bells was raised. In some cases this took so long that west towers were not yet finished at the eve of Reformation, and remain so.

Every tower was equipped with bells. They summoned clerks and people to services and offices – the first bell 'peal' being sounded before dawn – the angelus was rung three times a day from the main tower and the sanctus bell was rung, often from its own turret, at the consecration. Inventories made under Edward VI show that some churches had mighty bells of up to several tons in weight. One supposes that these all had differing functions, depending on the 'solemnity' of the occasion at which they were to be rung. Large bells were fixed and struck with iron clappers swung inside them, but it seems possible to me that smaller ones – such as the sanctus bells – might have been swung in imitation of the action of ringing a smaller hand-bell, the sort used in the sanctuary. However, though I am not a bell expert, I would comment that the history of the transition of bell-ringing practices, leading to modern peal-ringing, through the Reformation period is not clear and needs more documentary research. Certainly the practice of turning swinging bells so as to be able to sound them in predetermined sequences went through a longer evolution than seems to be generally supposed ; pre-Reformation CWA already mention wheels for bells, for instance. But once peal-ringing became established – as an outlet for social and para-musical activities otherwise closed down by the reformers, I suppose – technical changes necessary at their tops in order to hold bells while they were turned through nearly a circle meant a fairly rapid end to the majority of medieval bells.

How the Church was used

The main function of the *ecclesia* was to house the population that wished to attend daily services (Matins/Lauds, Mass and Vespers) and those that the whole parish was obliged to attend on Sundays. These offices and services were held for the most part in the eastern parts. Occasional services, specifically required by the people, were held in the western part and included christenings (which needed a porch and a font), weddings (porch and central alley) and funerals (the whole *ecclesia*).

To this general necessity was added over the centuries the need to extend the building with alleys for processions on the model of monastic 'naves', and with towers sturdy enough for numerous bells. Church wardens needed somewhere to keep tools such as mattocks for grave-digging and other maintenance equipment such as scythes, grappling hooks in case of fire in the thatch, equipment for scouring tiles or slates and gutters, and rakes and brushes for clearing old rushes and herbs from floors before laying down new ones.

The upper storey of church porches, many of which have lost their floors but still show signs of their access staircases, seem to have been used above all to keep the archives of the wardens and their money chests secure. Their windows are therefore small and well-barred ; where windows are larger it is possible that they were used as schools, and there are some with fireplaces. Porches in general deserve profound and widespread research, but it is clear that they were not places where people lived, as seems to be commonly supposed.

A priest in the Church

The parish priest had a complex job ; not only did he have to sing the daily round of services and regulate all aspects of the church's ceremonial life but he was also charged from the moment he took possession of the benefits of his position with the care of all the souls in his parish. He was the doctor in a temple of healing. Coming through the barrier-screen or round the church into a porch from the chancel door, he read those services needed by his parishioners for the better organising of their lives here and hereafter. These were the sacraments of baptism, a rite equal in importance with the mass, and the lesser sacraments of absolution, marriage, the bringing to church in thanksgiving of women after the perils of childbirth, and funeral rites.

All of these were partly or wholly performed in the *ecclesia*, and in English. Indeed, the churching rite (is this ever used now ?) in the first Common Prayer Books was almost exactly the late-medieval one, though the funeral rites were changed radically. Baptism was also stripped of practically all of the symbolism carefully woven into its rites, from the use of previously-hallowed water to the suppression of the use of chrisms (holy waxes and oils) and candles of various kinds. Although some of these have made a gradual come-back in the last half-century, as with almost everything that goes on now in church services the vital and memorable elements of drama have not made a re-appearance, as if we are too frightened to be marked by as well as to mark the inevitable chapters of life and death.

Competence and competition

In a spirit of competition that becomes clearer in CWA especially towards the end of the C14, there was also the question of doing the job of 'maintaining God's service' better than neighbouring parishes while still fulfilling the functional needs of complex liturgies such as those for Palm Sunday and the rest of the week that leads up to Easter day. Doing better included providing the finest churchyard crosses and Easter sepulchres, the brightest clerestories to light the rood and the nave generally, the astonishing late-medieval 'angel' and other magnificent roofs, the most ornate west façades and doorways to the tower, the tallest spires and the most profuse and gracious pinnacles. And as much interior and exterior sculpture in wood and stone as could be afforded.

Medieval English churches exhibit so many amazing feats of construction that we are all too inclined to take them for granted. But anyone with the slightest acquaintance with the principles of structural engineering will appreciate the detailed planning, encyclopaedic knowledge and almost infinite care needed at every stage of church constructions. Experience and education and a desire to be daring are crucial to the preparation and placing of hundreds of tons of oak to form a new late-medieval roof, with more hundreds of tons of lead placed on that, or the raising of a tall rural tower and spire like that at Clifton Campville in Staffordshire which stands on just four legs with apparently minimal support. It is obvious nonsense to suppose that these exploits, repeated over and again in our medieval churches, can have been done either by uneducated yokels or by bishops or monks. The people who created our churches were skilled and daring professionals, always pushing at the limits of technology, whether they were builders and sculptors, stained glass workers, carpenters and joiners, organ makers, metal workers and founders, scribes, illuminators or composers. These all worked within well-established international networks, both for their training and for the supply of skilled workers and widely-sourced products they needed for their work.

Medieval death

The spirit of parochial competition that made all this possible was not confined to active lives. Indeed, the rank one had in life would be publicly expressed in the manner of the burial and memorialising of the dead person. Most people would be buried at quite low cost (paid under its insurance system by their guild) in unmarked graves in the church's consecrated yard. Still-born children or those that died for any reason unbaptised were often buried under eaves so that rain could drop like tears over their technically non-Christian graves. Those of later years who could afford it might have some choice as where to be buried and a surprising number wished to be buried near or inside porches. The west side of later medieval towers were often built with knapped flints (which glint when they catch the sun) and were highly ornamented with dark flints set into white stonework as letters or other patterns. This side of the tower was intended to be a visual reminder of the splendid Palm Sunday ritual of Jesus' entry into Jerusalem. (Why quite a few churches do not have west doors is a puzzle that I would like an answer to but, as we have seen, explanations of things not still there or why they were never there does not seem to have been an interest of historians up to now.) Porches, especially the south one, were used for part of the marriage ceremony and a burial there even without a tomb-slab would be a strong signal for the person buried there to be remembered by generations of brides and grooms and their families. At Salle in Norfolk, the less-used north porch was (perhaps deliberately ?) given more cachet by having the church's Lady chapel in its upper loft or storey, so it may be that there were burials from porch to porch all round the west side of that church with its magnificent but incomplete tower.

The next stage up, and definitely more costly, both for the actual burial and then for the often huge dark-marble stones placed over them, was a burial in the centre alley of the church. This was, like the porches, a place of procession, most especially before the start of mass on Sundays and feast days when the host was solemnly carried along the alley for all to see and venerate it, passing over the remains of those fortunate enough to afford almost the top places in the building. But the really top places were in the chancel and they were reserved strictly for parish priests and lay founders of colleges. Those granted burial here seem to have one thing in common : that they had rebuilt the chancel itself or something equally spectacular. A chest-tomb for a priest is uncommon though, being usually reserved for an aristocratic founder or patron of substantial work.

Such subtle grading, and the constant reminders in bede biddings, died away when labelled as 'superstition' together with the reformation's complete change of theology over what constituted a Christian death. A 'dirge' or funeral mass was replaced by a service which failed either to commemorate the departed properly and to send him or her on their way or, emotionally vacant as it was, do much to support the bereaved with lovingly chosen words of care either. It has since been gradually eroded by the addition or substitution of eulogies and family tributes. However, one has attended such services where the attempt by clergy to 'humanise' this important event has resulted in toe-curling invitations to children to take part and in using expressions that fail to rise above the banal. Allan Wicks, the wonderfully wise, wacky and inimitable organist and master of the choristers at Canterbury cathedral from the 1960s to the 80s, said that a grand funeral ought to be a mixture of the military and the erotic. One can see where he was going : a fine service with all the ceremonial and music that can embellish a diligently prepared and performed funeral does have these elements, as anyone who remembers – who could forget ? – Lady Diana's last rites will know and cherish. Fortunately, Erasmus was right when he said that the English and their music would be hard to part : a church without fine music would be - and too often is – intellectually and often spiritually dead.

Perhaps to compensate for the poverty of funeral rites, and certainly because people were no longer memorial- ised in bede biddings, suddenly from the 1560s onwards memorials and tombs appear in profusion inside churches. From the 1660s onwards grave stones outside them also start to sprout from the grassy yard. Inside the church wall tablets appear for the first time and lay monuments start to appear in chancels, such as Shakespeare's at Stratford. Here his bust is where the college organ probably was, over an elaborate doorway that now leads nowhere. If wall tablets appear on the north wall of a former sanctuary they might cover evidence of an organ there, as we have seen ; others were placed over the former upper doorways of rood loft access stairways. The fashion for burials of all sorts of people inside churches brought income useful to church wardens trying, despite new church taxes levied on parishioners, to cope with ever-expanding non-religious demands. These burial vaults also brought disaster to the foundations of central towers of para-collegiate and college churches, which crashed with some frequency during the later C16 and early C17.

Pious graffiti

It has been realised quite recently that most of the scratches found on masonry in many more churches than had been previously identified have pious intent. When the columns of arches of all kinds were painted (as they were), such marks through the paint to the naked stone would be very visible.

A national study is still on-going, but enough has been found to show that these marks are visible prayers. A drawing of a ship for the safe return of cargo, of a knight for safety in war, of roses or daisies as prayers to Our Lady, are just some of the possible interpretations of signs whose full meaning has long ago gone out of memory. Why are there two drawings of medieval organs at Parham in Suffolk, for instance, when it is not (otherwise) even certain there were any organs there ?

Bosses and corbels

Studies on these are so far regional and need to be expanded nationwide. Those churches already studied in the west country suggest that iconographical schemes of undisturbed bosses are there to lead their viewers to consider their part in committing social and moral sins represented by these bosses, such as slander or vanity. They are then led to pass eastwards through the *ecclesia,* under the gaze of familiar faces, then taking strength from the examples of the saints in the rood-loft parapet and dado and the supreme example of salvation represented by the crucifix. Going towards the rood-screen also takes the penitent towards the sacrament of

absolution after confession heard through the same
screen (possibly through holes made for the purpose)
where at Easter parishioners, after careful and lengthy
preparation, would also receive communion.

Corbels represent another puzzle, unexplained for so
many generations that their meaning is almost totally
opaque for us, especially when they seem to be portraits
of people. The question is whether these are real people
– as they often seem to be – or representative 'types', or
both ? A similar sort of compound question can be posed
for almost everything we can still see from the medieval
period. The medieval mind was used to considering all
matters from various perspectives, without the 100%
literalness that we have come to expect after generations
of standardisation, and of portraiture and photography.
We rejoice in something being 'literal' (even if it isn't)
but the medieval mind preferred a deeper and wider
probing into everything it saw or read. It liked to see
connections at different layers of meaning, too, and
perhaps we should all be looking at medieval churches
with this in mind – they are connected buildings, each
detail being an essential part of the whole design both in
terms of conception and of decoration. We have a long

way to go before we can understand enough to know even where start to dig into these medieval mycellia.

Exterior chapels

The ME word 'chapel' means two things, the first being a separate church building designed to cater for a newly-established population some distance away from the parish church. The establishment of markets or new or enlarged ports often led to market and port towns being at some distance from their 'home' parish church, such as at Market Harborough in Leicestershire (a chapel of Great Bowden) or Needham Market in Suffolk (a chapel of Barking), Hythe in Kent (a chapel of Saltwood) or indeed Holy Trinity chapel in Hull and St Nicholas chapel in Lynn, these last two chapels being among the largest and finest of their kind. These chapels 'of ease' (as they were later called) did not have christening or burial rights but were places where services might be maintained by a full staff of clergy or a single *capellanus* or chaplain.

The other kind of chapel was a separate building in the churchyard or somewhere else in the parish that was for

instance near to a well (ME for spring) or to the grave or
shrine of a local saint, or was in the proximity of a 'new'
(i.e. not manorial) great house – such as the Clopton's
chapel in southern Long Melford. There were two
chapels in the church yards of Faversham parish church
in Kent and High (Cheaping) Wycombe in Buckinghamshire, and a perhaps surprising number of other more
modest parishes also had separate chapels in their yards.
Major town guilds also built their own chapels in town
centres, but so did rural guilds, as at for instance Pulham
St Mary in Norfolk. We may be aware of the apparent
proliferation of manorial chapels in, for instance,
Brittany, but Britain was no laggard in this respect,
though the extent of these has yet to be researched
thoroughly and published.

Priests' and clerks' housing

Not much research has been done towards establishing
precisely how many priests' and clerks' or chanters'
houses still remain in Britain, but those that survive in
something like their original form, as at Muchelney in
Somerset and Kingsbeare in Devon, show them to be

substantial. The general opinion of those few who have studied them is that they were graded from large yeoman-style houses for rector-priests down to smaller houses for vicars. Such grading was natural, since it was the priest of the time who was expected to maintain his house unless he had other arrangements with the rector. He also shared his house with auxiliary priests such as the chantry or other stipendiary priests and guests. One of the duties of a parish priest was to feed and shelter wayfarers on the lines of the same charity expected of monasteries.

Guilds – halls and plays

Another aspect of medieval life that needs far more study on the ground throughout England and Wales is the vast influence that guilds, both religious and craft (as far as these can be separated, which they were in actual practice only after 1547), had in both parochial and political life. As in other aspects of medieval life, guilds are complex and difficult to define, existing at many different levels and fulfilling a large number of tasks. These included including protection of crafts, family insurance, the formation of large trade networks, and the establishment and maintenance of dedicated chantry altars where prayers for the well-being of the souls of their departed sisters and brethren were intended to be 'perpetually' sung. They also naturally had a hand in education, guild halls or guild chapels being often schools as well, or (as at Stratford) schools being built and – until their lands were taken away by Edward VI, that non-schoolbuilder – maintained by the aldermen of the town who were at the same time high functionaries in their guilds.

No doubt the same functionaries influenced the church wardens, if they were not one and the same, when it came to putting on plays and the processions in towns using pageants (ME for floats, each with its own scenery and players sponsored by a particular guild). We have some of the texts of these plays - those that survived governmental disapproval, fearing unreliable public assembly – and they provide, like the CWA, excellent insights into how English was spoken at that time. Did the same church wardens allow the players to carry on up the stairs beyond porch lofts onto the lead roofs of aisles to stage, in full view of a crowd below in the grave-free yard, miracles of the Annunciation, Resurrection, Transfiguration and Assumption ? I can't help hoping they did, and we do know that at Worcester abbey in the C13 boys did precisely this sort of thing, climbing up into parts of the building and probably descending on wires to represent doves and angels.

At Wells cathedral the Palm Sunday re-enactment of the entry into Jerusalem included boys and trumpeters hidden behind statues to breathe life into them. A spectacular play on a south alley roof on a sunny day with an ale-feast at its close would make an entertainment worthy of the invitations to neighbouring parishes that we know were sent out, and would provide substantial funds for the church and its greater glorification.

Church houses

Another separate building, this one usually bordering or not far away from the church yard, was the church house, meaning the house belonging to the *ecclesia*, the people. Again, there were many more of these than is apparent now, most of then having been sold off in hard times. There were two chief problems with them for later Tudor governments : they were, like plays, places of public assembly and therefore potential breeding grounds for discontent, and, shockingly, ale was brewed there for the support of the church. Some of the buildings were privatised into public houses ; those with such names as 'The Angel and Harp' or 'Five Bells' and their proximity to the church might indicate their real origins. A full national study of church houses has yet to be carried out.

Church houses had been built from the mid-C15 onwards and their repair and upkeep is frequently the cause of recorded expenditure by church wardens in their accounts. They were built as all-season meeting places ; they could lodge guests or house long-term tenants, they were where people could bake bread (and perhaps if necessary the holy loaf that was blessed and distributed at the end of mass) and where ales were brewed for feasts at Easter, for patronal festivals, and for sale at fairs and at plays.

Conclusion

The future use of chancels

If a chancel ever regains its primary medieval purpose as the place for worship, once the nave, the peoples' part, finally reverts to the local community for non-religious purposes, then its future use needs to be reviewed with care. One might even ask if this part of the church should remain as the only charge on the worshipping community - what Churchill called the pillars of the church - while the rest of the building is sustained by the community at large, people characterised by Churchill (as he described himself) as flying buttresses.

The Sustainability Review did not propose this as a possible solution. One might doubt if it was ever discussed, for fear of the potential problems that it would stir up. Certainly any demarcation issues will have to be dealt with, but it is clear that these were handled for the most part with care and discretion during the 600 or so years during which a distinction between chancel and church was integral to the management of the building, as we have seen. There is a long-term, tried and tested, model that might be followed. All it needs is for church and community to pull together and in the same direction.

As far as one can tell from surviving documents, demarcation conflicts in medieval churches are far rarer than unrevised apologists for the Reformation – and its proponents at the time – have tried to make us believe. Once it was made clear who was responsible for what in a church (as we saw above, this had been done in the early C13) then the margin for such conflict was narrowed. In fact, their accounts very often seem to suggest that church wardens, on behalf of their parishioners, actually furnished more than they really needed to, and guilds added even more to the 'store' of church goods in both parts of the church building.

If such a division of responsibilities was undertaken again, then two major matters will need to be resolved. First, those who use the chancel will have to undertake to do so with understanding and respect for its history and remaining artefacts. As perhaps this essay has made clear, we are on the whole far from having a deep and full appreciation of these places. In our researches, we have seen some horrible things done to chancels, ranging from neglect to filling it with carpets and comfortable chairs and sofas, or storing ladders along choir seats. The back and sides of organs are all too often used as dumping places and vestries are full of tacky objects, and rood screens have electrical and plumbing holes bored through them or power point screens placed on top of them.

Some dignity will have to be restored to this part of the church. As more than one church warden has told us, chancels would be the ideal place for holding services for the small congregations that come expecting not to freeze during winter services. One actually mentioned this just before – following quite a bit of persuasion – she showed us a former chantry chapel (previously unreported, despite the fame of the church) full of the sort of things one would normally expect to find in a large broom cupboard. It was large enough to take a congregation of up to twenty people, apparently the usual number that sat in the enormous chancel next to it for winter-time services. However such a place would have to be very carefully treated and furnished before being used frequently – it maintains an amazing amount of its original painted decoration, some of its fixtures and even some frescoes – although the advantages of doing this are obvious. Each church in fact would need very careful guidance from well-informed future CSAs and

FCOs on the future use and furnishing of the eastern parts of their building.

Architects and others concerned with the refurbishment of churches – which these days can include creating new rooms within a nave, having removed all pews and put down new floors with under-floor heating – need to be aware of two effects this work might have. One is the change to the acoustic qualities of the building that these might make ; sometimes for the better if the floor is left with a hard finish, often not as the space becomes smaller and differently shaped. The other is the effect on organs : such work often finds organs 'in the way' and they are removed, even if historically important or otherwise worthwhile instruments. A more insidious problem is that underfloor heating gradually dries out the building. When humidity levels drop to around 40%, organs are potentially in trouble. How much they are affected will depend on their position, size, materials and construction. Well-trained, impartial and experienced advice is needed – and this is currently in short supply.

The future of organs

The second major difficulty regarding the rethinking of the chancel might be the existing organ, though like everything else a problem can be turned to advantage if it is seen as challenging rather than insuperable. One issue is that during the last 50 years or so, many organs have been moved out of chancels into naves at a time when the recent steep decline in especially rural and suburban congregations was not anticipated. Moving organs has opened up some space, and unblocked light from southern windows, in chancels that could well do with both of these improvements, though some of these spaces have since been used for less than worthy purposes, as mentioned above. Again, dealing with organs will have to be handled with care, taking each case individually. But some general points might be made, using the experience gained from a life-time working with organs and from what we have seen in our research.

If an organ is on the north side of the chancel, and is not too complicated or large (this generally means an organ built before 1900 and with no more than about 15 stops) then it should be possible to keep this in situ and maintain it there. A smaller organ, such as one of the many 'chancel organs' made following the Revd John Baron's influential 1850s book on 'Scudamore' organs, or a former house organ that has been recycled at some time into the church, should be kept for its potential or actual intrinsic merits. English organ builders from around 1780 until the 1860s had a huge experience of making really effective smaller organs with the most advanced techniques available. They were then far ahead of continental makers, though this was thanks partly to new ways of organising workshops pioneered by 'Swiss mechanics'. (Making organs continued to be, and still is, often an international profession.) Organs of this period are therefore generally very well made and can always be restored to last for at least another 125 years or so before needing major work again.

Many church wardens now speak of 'having to attract organists', in what has become a time of scarcity of players. In fact, all too often churches are themselves to blame for this situation. In the past, relationships between truculent organists who feel themselves undervalued and parish priests who have no musical training, or any real interest in the wealth of music which might be at their disposal, have often gone sour when if properly guided and mutually encouraged a strong and effective team could have resulted. The other major reason for the lack of organists is what has seemed to have been a relentless driving out of choirs, by ignorant clergy, from churches over the last 40 years. As a result, young singers who might have – as used very often to be the case –graduated to playing the organ have simply not been given that possibility. (The same clergy complain, of the lack of young people in their church ...) Community choirs should to be set up (again) in as many churches as possible, but this time not necessarily to sing at services, even if they might do so occasionally, so that a virtuous cycle of musical and personal training can be restored.

One way out of the impasse has been to 'attract' organists by offering them an organ of their dreams. This offers an enormous temptation to a player who does not always have the experience to know what a good and appropriate organ is or to be able play one with taste or discretion. (Or with surprise and seduction, the essence of music of all kinds.) It lands the church with either a large electronic organ with a self-limited life or a very substantial pipe organ of the neo-romantic kind still favoured – and paid for at huge expense – by most large churches and almost all cathedrals.

This is not a caricature ; in our research we have seen the effect of all these adventures. It is as if no-one has ever heard of the artistic saying that 'more is less, and less more'. Anyway, if rural medieval chancels are going to become again self-contained units, large organs that encumber them might well be replaced with smaller ones, especially one of the many available ones from the golden period mentioned above, but also from present-day organ makers, who heaven knows need some

imaginative encouragement of their amazing but
perilously-endangered skills.

Any organist 'not able' to play such a smaller organ – it is
indeed more difficult to find out everything that a small
organ can give, needing imagination and commitment –
is not actually likely to be able to play a larger one
imaginatively either. Unfortunately, there does seem to
be a general reluctance to accept 'second-hand' organs ;
this is seen as second best, whereas if judged well by
competent, trained advisers and open-minded organ
makers it can be a first-best and long-term solution.

An historical organ should be treated with the same
respect as any other historic fixture in a church. (Organs
are really fixtures, and should be treated as such in legis-
lation too, another issue that needs to be sorted out in
the wake of the Sustainability Review.) A good organ of
any date needs to be seen as a plus for the church which
has the good fortune to have one, and the capital value it
represents should be exploited to the full. Imaginative
'other' uses for organs, not only for services but for
concerts with any other kind of instrument, or solo voice
or choir– rôles a good English organ performs better
than any other type – need to be fostered. Sometimes
this might be easier in churches such as those managed
by the Churches Conservation Trust, the Historic
Churches Trust or Friends of Friendless Churches and
other similar organisations. Some of their churches that
do not already have organs might be appropriate places
to put otherwise unwanted organs, where they can be
used for teaching, concerts and played as extra
attractions in flower festivals and during open or special
visiting days.

Organ builders constantly moan about their work being
under-esteemed, but they could do something about this
if asked to show and explain what they do. An ideal time
to do this is at craft demonstrations which obviously
should include the high-standard craft of making and
restoring organs as well as all the other special skills that
go into building and adorning churches. I would also say
that organists could play their part in presenting organs

well by keeping their music tidy – possibly a lost cause !
– and their (cleaned) keyboards open to view. Visitors
could also be initiated in the fascinating mystery of
organs in general and in any particular example if the
player puts up a simple notice which describes in non-
technical language the salient and interesting features of
the organ concerned. I would go further and suggest that
churches and the diocese and their staff and advisers
(future FCOs and CSAs) should also make real efforts to
see that an organ is presented as well as any other fine
piece of furniture and as such kept in as good dust-free
and appropriately-polished order as, for instance, an
eagle lectern might be.

When I have worked in large houses, visitors have often
said to me how much they appreciate the extra element
that 'live music' music played on organs or pianos
introduces to their enjoyment of these buildings. It is, or
can be, the same in churches. Playing a few contrasting
and appropriate pieces on the organ for ten minutes
before a service too would set the scene for what was to
follow far better than the rushing around of last-minute
preparations that all too often actually happens in
poorly-led churches. (Cathedral organists could also do
something about playing something more worthy than
mediocre or worse 'improvisations' before their services.)
Even in churches which do not use organs much during
the services, congregations could still be reminded of the
existence of their major capital and aesthetic asset in this
way, too. England's churches are full of small and
charming instruments which need to be heard, using the
enormous repertory available for such organs, not least
the English one which has loveable music suitable for all
levels of playing attainment, some written (as by John
Marsh) with budding 'practicioners' in mind.

Opening churches

It is still necessary to repeat here what so many
researchers and lovers of churches have said : that
although there have been many very welcome efforts

made to open churches and invite visitors, there are still churches that remain locked and all too often without any contact numbers for even a persistent visitor to gain entrance. Some churches even manage to put such notices inside a porch and then lock its outside door-grille, rendering the notice unreadable ! Perhaps not all church communities feel able to offer a welcome on the scale of the notoriously disestablished church of Mickfield in Suffolk, where visitors are invited to help themselves to tea or coffee in the south porch as they go in, but it would be wonderful if large notices that say 'Welcome to our church' are backed up with an unlocked door. Our experience has been that, ridiculously, the opposite is often the case.

The crucial point to make is that if churches are to be sustainable, they have to be available as well, especially to their own communities. English churches have never belonged solely to their congregations but to all their parishioners ; this is the essence of the parochial system which if wisely exploited might go a long way to making them sustainable again. It is perfectly clear that in medieval times churches were sustained by everyone, whatever their private thoughts about points of doctrine.

If admission to churches now is only by adherence to a sectarian view – whether evangelical or high-church – and the rest are kept out, these churches are sooner or later doomed to die. Those in charge of dioceses must stop being feebly complaisant in allowing sectarian groups to take over what is essentially public property.

Insurance of churches is not an excuse for locking them either ; most insurers agree that it is better to keep churches open, one remarking to me, 'It's better that thieves go in through the door than through a stained glass window'. Simple video surveillance systems are not expensive and most people are no longer shocked by being filmed by CCTV cameras. Important items in churches can be kept in safe places – as most church plate already is – or simply screwed down effectively.

Festival churches

A specious phrase to describe churches that it is proposed will be closed for worship other than on or around major feasts (described as Christmas, Easter and Harvest), or on demand for weddings, funerals or baptisms. It is promised that such churches will be open 'during the day', which might be an improvement, but almost all other aspects of the proposal are worryingly neither thought through or pragmatic. Matters of insurance, and who precisely will be ultimately financially responsible for these churches are not clear, though in some areas such churches are already being nominated, as for instance in Oxford, Truro and Lincoln dioceses. Lincoln diocese had indeed a terrible record for absentee clergy; as late as 1852 nearly half of its parishes in its home county still did not have resident, beneficed clergy. Its own bishop wrote in 1849 that Lincoln county went 'beyond any other that furnishes instances of pluralities, of non-residence and of insufficient performance of the services'. One has to wonder if the Mickfield example cited above may not have to be followed *de facto* if not *de jure*, to the horror of church administrators. The rôle of CSAs and FCOs could be vital here, but not if they are going to stifle local initiative with even more diocesan bureaucracy of the kind whose mere mention provoked frustrated *cris du coeur* from many of the church wardens we met during our researches. It is promised to perform services in Festival Churches 'to a high standard' (as if that was not already a given) but how an organ that has been left unplayed during damp winter months will be at a high standard on the infrequent occasions it is needed is far from clear, unless the said CSAs and FCOs are taught basic maintenance skills and pass them on in turn to local volunteers.

Envoi

All those churches we have been looking at and trying to understand were once the churches of the people, and perhaps one day they will be once again. A C19 bishop, returning from his colonial see to spend his retirement in transcribing and publishing church wardens' accounts in Somerset and elsewhere, felt able to summarise what his labours had unearthed thus :

'In nearly all the documents illustrating parish life of, say, the fifteenth century, there is evidence of the community of purpose of pastor and people which is really astounding.'

Another C19 historian wrote :

'The immense treasures in the churches were the joy and boast of every man and woman and child in England, who, day by day and week by week, assembled to worship in the old houses of God which they and their fathers had built, and whose every vestment and chalice, and candlestick and banner, organ and bells, and pictures and images, and altar and shrine, they looked upon as their own, and part of their birthright.'

These then were the community's treasures, celebrated and memorialised from that pulpit, placed a few yards down the church from the rood screen, which was at the centre of the opening scene in this book. Five hundred

years later, the stock of treasure is rather different –
more an accumulation of social events during that time
than things strictly dedicated to the 'increase of worship'
- but it still makes England's medieval churches worth
sustaining with all the effort of which we are capable,
while also trying to understand them better than ever.

This book will be launched 17 February 2018 at the annual British Institute of Organ Studies research conference at the Barber Institute on Birmingham University campus. Here, ten years ago, a 'simple question' – 'How many organs were there in English churches in 1500 ?' - was posed by BIOS chairman and professor of music, Dr Peter Williams. He would certainly not have agreed with everything written in this book, nor the way in which it is expressed, but would I think have cherished the idea that his question should have encouraged a much closer look at some things that we might previously have thought we knew something about.

Our research has taken us to more than 800 churches, to investigate them carefully, make measured sketches and many photographs. Three other books, based on our research, will be published in due course, the first, entitled 'Seven Whole Days : music and education in the medieval church', a detailed work with full documentary support, of which this present book is a short distillation, a second book of detailed case-studies of selected churches, and a book specifically on the history of the organ in England from around 1300 to 1600. For further information, including lectures and other essays, visit soundsmedieval.org, where comments, bouquets and brickbats will be welcomed.